TEACHER'S HANDBOOK FOR A
FUNCTIONAL BEHAVIOR-BASED CURRICULUM

Communicable Models and Guides
for Classroom Use

TEACHER'S HANDBOOK FOR A
FUNCTIONAL BEHAVIOR-BASED CURRICULUM

*Communicable Models and Guides
for Classroom Use*

Sidney J. Drumheller
Drake University

Educational Technology Publications
Englewood Cliffs, New Jersey 07632

Printed in the United States of America.

Library of Congress Catalog Card Number: 72-933.

International Standard Book Number: 0-87778-036-6.

First printing.

To my wife Kae and my children—Susan, Mark, and Craig

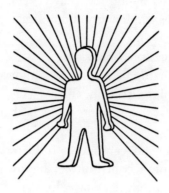

PREFACE

The behavioral objectives movement of the last two decades has made all school faculties aware of the vagueness of their aims and curricular designs. While many teachers have successfully repressed their findings, or have learned to live quite happily with guilt feelings, others have attempted to justify old teaching patterns by tortuously contriving behavioral objectives to *fit*, or have rewritten their courses to follow a logical behavioral focus. For the most part, these courses of action have been neither satisfying nor effective because of the dehumanizing, sterile barriers they often create between the teacher and the learner. The objective has defined an atomized piece of behavior the teacher is to nurture which will ultimately be combined with other pieces to form a functional behavior—a behavior, however, of which the teacher is presently unaware.

This book has been developed with the assumption that both teacher and learner should be aware, from the beginning of instruction, of the *global behaviors* the learner is aspiring to attain. As the *component behaviors* are attacked, they are performed in context so they remain both meaningful and functional throughout instruction.

The behaviors required of an individual in dealing with his

environment and with himself have been divided into four categories to give the whole curriculum direction and thrust:

1. social behaviors,
2. communications behaviors,
3. self-actualizing behaviors which give the individual's life meaning and direction, and
4. manipulative behaviors which harness the physical world.

The individual who can successfully operate in each of the four domains can be a contributing, happy member of society. Because the social studies, language, humanities, and math-science subjects (or disciplines) of the school roughly correspond to the four behavior domains, the proposed pattern for curriculum development is compatible with content-based patterns existing in today's schools.

A chapter has been devoted to each of the four behavior categories. In each a "map" is developed which charts the learner's developmental needs, and suggests curricular areas with which the teacher should be concerned. The maps are simple enough to be committed to memory or posted to guide cooperative planning efforts.

Basic to the thrust of this book is the notion that both teachers and students should be designers, artisans, and workers, and not simply robots painting or piling up bricks by the numbers. The global maps define and justify the major instructional programs, while the particular behavioral deficiencies of the learners define and justify the rudimentary behaviors to be shaped. The learner does *not* progress by blindly mastering a series of isolated behaviors and fitting them together into a functional whole. Instead, he attempts to perform the larger behavior; he identifies his shortcomings; and he shapes his deficiencies within the framework of the larger performance.

While this approach is clearly advocated by behavioral psychologists, most school learning programs ignore it. Most learners and teachers need this perspective to keep the learning experiences *alive and vital.* Short, mechanical programs can be periodically inserted, but only if the learner's perspective is preserved.

This book explores some of the problems involved in implementing such a behavioral focus in the 1970s. A plan for a stable transitional curriculum, where teachers can develop new materials and teachers and learners can adjust to a functional, behavior-based curriculum, is explored and offered as a hopeful remedy for ordering what is today the chaotic field of behavioral objectives.

The writer has published or is soon to publish portions of this book in a variety of books and periodicals.

Chapter One is adapted from an article in *Educational Horizons,* December, 1967, entitled, "The School's Responsibility to Society and to the Individual."

Chapter Two is adapted from the second chapter of *Handbook of Curriculum Design for Individualized Instruction: A Systems Approach,* Educational Technology Publications, Englewood Cliffs, New Jersey, 1971.

A modified version of Chapter Three will be published by *NASSP Bulletin* (National Association of Secondary School Principals).

Chapter Four is adapted from an article in *Educational Technology,* September, 1971, entitled, "Behavioral Objectives for the Social Studies in General Education."

Chapter Five is adapted from an article in *Elementary English,* February, 1969, entitled, "Objectives for Language Arts in Nongraded Schools."

Sidney J. Drumheller

TABLE OF CONTENTS

TEACHER'S HANDBOOK FOR A FUNCTIONAL BEHAVIOR-BASED CURRICULUM

Communicable Models and Guides
for Classroom Use

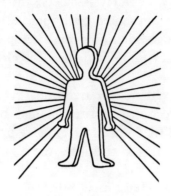

PART I

A RATIONALE FOR A
BEHAVIOR-BASED CURRICULUM

Twentieth century school critics have attacked public education and educators from a multitude of fortified positions with a multitude of grievances. Scholars have criticized the schools' lack of scholarship. Scientists have criticized the schools' lack of system in providing for the step-by-step development of the scientific perspective. Humanists have argued that the schools lack concern for the nurturing of the unique *human* qualities in an individual. The educational technologist complains that educators are not applying the knowledge, strategies, and technology that have already been proved effective in education. The list could be extended indefinitely. This volume develops a position which is *compatible with each of the above.* It offers an educational umbrella under which all could thrive, focusing on the nurturing of a self-fulfilled, contributing citizen.

The book is divided into three parts. Part I—A Rationale for a Behavior-Based Curriculum—describes the behavioral position, the need for it, and the opposition to it. Part II—Four Maps for Charting a School's Curriculum—identifies the real-life behaviors needed by a learner in today's society; these are the behaviors from which a curriculum should get its perspective. Part III—Bringing About the Change—identifies some key pitfalls in the change process, and presents some guidelines for effective implementation.

Chapter One examines the traditional role of the school as a supplementary educational institution and baby-sitting service, nurturing the three Rs in children growing up in three relatively healthy behavior-shaping institutions—the family, the church, and the community.

The functional educational roles of these institutions are currently being abdicated at alarming rates, and the schools are not tooled to take up the slack. The school, however, is the only institution powerful and knowledgeable enough to take on the job of helping the child to solve the problems with which he is confronted in today's environment.

Chapter Two—An Instructional Lifeline: Global Behavioral Objectives—orients the educator to the behavioral objective and how it can guide him in making education functional.

Chapter Three—Behavioral Objectives and the Academic Disciplines—shows the philosophical relationship between the knowledge taught in the traditional classroom and the knowledge required by the citizen problem-solver. Here a rationale is developed which allows both the traditionalist and the behaviorist to live under the same umbrella.

CHAPTER ONE

THE ROLE OF THE SCHOOL:
REAL AND IDEAL

When the Sputnik panic button was pushed by Congress in 1957, federal funds suddenly became available for any educational dream projects which could stir the imagination of the funding agency. "Educational Innovation" became synonymous with educational progress.

After almost two decades of ferment the balloon has burst, the funds have dried up, and the wreckage of countless educational projects is everywhere. An economic recession from 1969 to 1972 did much to reinforce the nation's accountability-minded groups in their struggle to cut unnecessary taxes and streamline publicly administered services.

There are many still arguing, with Arthur Bestor, that our schools are educational wastelands. A few of the more optimistic feel that "accountability" could be a reality "next semester" if only we would put forth a little effort.

The danger in this emphasis, as with any popular educational movement, is that the key terms will be applied so broadly that they will become meaningless. In the sense that we are using it, "accountability" focuses on the individual school.

As Henry S. Dyer (1970) says, accountability embraces three general principles:

> 1. The professional staff of a school is to be held collectively responsible for *knowing* as much as it can (a) about the intellectual and personal-social development of the pupils in its charge and (b) about the conditions and educational services that may be facilitating or impeding the pupils' development.

> 2. The professional staff of a school is to be held collectively responsible for *using* this knowledge as best it can to maximize the development of its pupils toward certain clearly defined and agreed-upon pupil performance objectives.

> 3. The board of education has a corresponding responsibility to provide the means and technical assistance whereby the staff of each school can acquire, interpret, and use the information necessary for carrying out the two foregoing functions.

The crux of the accountability problem lies in the implied contract in principle two. The traditional school has no clearly defined performance objectives, and it is against its survival interest to open such a Pandora's Box. Its initial attempt in the direction will involve the citing of such objectives as:

The learner will:

1. diagram any English sentence in terms of a Latin format;
2. identify the major generals in the Second Punic War when asked.

As soon as all parties agree on a reasonably complete package, the meaninglessness of the total school function becomes apparent—most of the goals are abstract, discipline-oriented tidbits that neither the teacher nor the child can perceive as *functional*. The teachers, however, have a lifetime commitment to this game. Even when a faculty recognizes that functional pupil behaviors should be the focus of education, the majority of teachers are neither inclined nor trained to meet such demands.

The faculty is thus faced with the dilemma of either guiltily teaching the old way, knowing there is a better one, or quitting. Unless this chasm can be bridged, accountability efforts will be doomed to frustration and failure.

Let us explore some rationales for curriculum building in the 1970s that will enable schools to be functionally accountable to realistic behavioral objectives, yet be flexible enough to allow teachers to perform within their style and motivational limitations.

What is the function of the school? It keeps some 20 million adolescents and post-adolescents off the job market. The school "Americanizes" millions of culturally deprived and foreign-born children. It provides child care at public expense for 45 million minors, giving them organized activities, and keeping them off the streets. This is not to say that this is all the school does, but these things alone might well justify its existence.

The school usually claims to develop the academic skills and attitudes which are prerequisites to vocational success and "the preservation of the American way." The assumption is that neither goal is attainable without formal schooling. But is this true?

If all primary schools were closed tomorrow for a ten-year period, would we have a generation of children unable to read, write, or compute? Probably not. It is likely that many, if not most, children would master the skills simply because society demanded it of them, while the remainder would probably fall quite short in reading and writing, but achieve in arithmetic, because of the demands of the economic system. Probably even better results would be found in teaching about health, the family, the neighborhood, and current events, because of an increased mobility in the population and more contact with mass media—especially television. If the above speculations are true, it would mean that many of the avowed objectives of the traditional elementary school are actually "mopping-up" exercises, in which the school simply increases society's batting average in teaching the child the skills needed to survive in, and perpetuate, a free society.

In recent years an ever-increasing proportion of state and federal funds has been supporting the local schools, making them more and more independent of local control. This tends to make the school a kind of island in the culture, with its own government and its own concerns. It enables the school to restate its objectives in terms of both the needs of tomorrow's child and the needs of tomorrow's society.

The writer feels that the freeing of the local school from the financial whims of the community and the shifting of educational leadership from political to professional hands is a step forward. However, the school must remain an institution of the regional culture and periodically show evidence of its worth. Bridges must be built to the island.

Now, can we identify the new functions of this changing institution? While the roles mentioned above are concerned with the preservation of the status quo, the new role focuses upon the building of something different. While the former can be done rather routinely by following already-established paths, the latter requires imagination, systematic analysis, careful research, and synthesis of research findings. Let us first recognize that our society wants its youth off the employment market and off the streets, and it looks to the school for this service. Second, let us recognize that most of the institutions of society have their own educational devices, so that the school's role in the acculturation process is more closely related to the task of *mixing* children than *teaching* them, in order that those who have not been educated by the cultural institutions can learn from those who have. Third, let us recognize that when we attempt to formally indoctrinate children into the culture, we are likely to succeed only if we are attempting a "mopping-up" exercise rather than a basic training program. And fourth, let us recognize that many children are motivated to participate in school activities through a concern for acceptance and approval—adult acceptance in the primary school, yielding to peer acceptance in the intermediate school. This, rather than the worth of the content, accounts for the learner's participation.

Although the culture with which the adult identifies is relatively stable from day to day, the child alternately identifies with two cultures—the society of children and the larger culture.

L. Joseph Stone and Joseph Church (1957) compare the attributes of the "society of children" to the folkways and rituals of primitive cultures which are handed down by word of mouth from generation to generation, whose meanings have often been lost but are extremely resistant to extinction.

> In one sense the peer group affiliation of the middle years, the immersion in being a child, looks like a detour on the road to maturity. From another standpoint, however, it appears as a necessary and valuable stage in the process of finding one's own identity . . . He is ready to begin the quest for an independent existence . . . This "detour" then is an essential moving away from the parents in which a genuine and separate identity can be formed . . .

The child lives in a world of fascinating stimuli, any of which could serve as learning experiences. Some of the stimuli are deliberately ordered, so as to enhance learning, as in the classroom and in the mass media. Others are ordered by "human nature." The individual does not notice and participate in the experience until he is ready, developmentally. Most stimuli go unnoticed, because they are irrelevant to the child's needs and experiences. A child living in the center of a megalopolis with a good TV antenna might be able to select stimuli from a dozen TV channels, two or three neighborhood gangs, a variety of good literature, pop music, classical music, the refrigerator, the newspaper, comic books, and so forth. Opportunities for learning are all about him, waiting for his participation. His tendency, however, is to reach closure too soon. He consistently seeks out "a gang," "a disc jockey," a few "top TV programs," "an author," day after day, as the society pressures him to conform to peer standards.

The role of the teacher was once compared to the role of the sweeper in the old Scottish game of curling. In the game a large, heavy stone is slid across the ice toward another stone. The sweepers sweep the ice in front of the moving stone to clear a path toward the goal. They don't want the stone to stop too soon. The cultural pressures acting upon the child encourage him to stop too soon.

Let us now explore a series of ideas which might help the school organize its efforts in shaping the child for tomorrow's society.

Robert J. Havighurst (1953) has defined a concept which he calls "the developmental task." The developmental task is "a task which arises at or about a certain period in the life of the individual, successful achievement of which leads to his happiness and to success with later tasks, while failure leads to unhappiness in the individual, disapproval by the society, and difficulty with later tasks." In this definition, five drives of the learner have been identified. These are happiness now, happiness later, approval now, approval later, and success later. This point of view again draws our attention to the dilemma faced by the educator who desires to make his objectives functional. While the learner is usually more concerned with happiness and approval now, the educator is usually more concerned with the child's happiness, approval, and success in the future. In fact the educator often feels that the child has reached closure too soon and that he is too happy in his present ignorant and blissful state, and that this closure should have been prevented.

Figure 1 portrays Havighurst's developmental tasks, from infancy through later adulthood. The writer has grouped these tasks into four functional categories of development: (1) social demands, (2) communications demands, (3) self-actualization demands, and (4) non-social environmental demands. As one traces the sequential pattern of development—for instance, social development—throughout the life span, note that the learning process is not clearly hierarchical, where the later behaviors are built from the earlier behaviors in a neat, orderly manner. The rebellious behavior of adolescence might be in direct conflict with the expected behavior of adulthood. The self-picture one strives to protect in adolescence or early adulthood is quite different from the one he protects in later adulthood.

While Havighurst has focused his attention on tasks demanded of all individuals in a culture, the writer would consider these as minimal performances for the less able learner. A developmental task for a prospective surgeon might focus on the ability to perform an appendectomy. Whereas many of Havighurst's tasks are nurtured almost completely by other institutions in the society, the tasks to be added to the list would be more exclusively the school's. This means that the emphasis would change from a "mopping-up" focus to a concern for the developing of the individual into the most effective adult possible in the areas described above.

Figure 2 portrays in general terms the educational pathways to be followed in the nurturing of developmental task performances throughout the life span. The four diagonal paths define the four task categories of communications, social problem-solving, self-actualization, and environmental problem-solving. At one end of the incline is the infant, neutral and naive, and at the other end are the developmental tasks the individual hopes to achieve when he reaches his adult prime. Most of these aspirations are never quite reached, and the individual finally detours from this path as he attempts to adjust to the problems of aging.

Figure 1

Developmental Tasks Throughout the Life Span
(From R.J. Havighurst, 1953)

	Tasks of Infancy and Early Childhood	Tasks of Later Childhood	Tasks of Adolescence	Tasks of Early Adulthood	Tasks of Middle Adulthood	Tasks of Later Adulthood
Social	Learning to relate one's self emotionally to parents, siblings, and other people; Learning to distinguish right from wrong and develop a conscience; Forming simple concepts of social reality	Learning to get along with age mates; Developing attitudes toward social groups and institutions; Learning appropriate masculine or feminine role; Developing conscience, morality; Learning physical skills necessary for ordinary games	Achieving new and more mature relations with age mates of both sexes; Achieving a masculine or feminine social role; Desiring and achieving socially responsible behavior; Preparing for marriage and family life; Developing intellectual skills and concepts necessary for civic competence	Selecting a mate and learning to live with him (her) ... or ... Establishing a way of living as a single person; (If married) Rearing children; Accepting civic responsibility; Finding congenial social group	(If married) Continuing to relate one's self to one's spouse as two individuals; Adjusting to aging parents; Achieving adult civic and social responsibilities	(If married) Preparing for and adjusting to eventual death of spouse; Establishing explicit affiliation with one's own age group
Communications	Learning to talk	Developing fundamental skills in reading, writing, and calculating				
Self-Actualization		Developing a scale of values; Building wholesome attitudes toward one's self as a growing organism; Achieving personal independence	Acquiring a set of values and an ethical system as a guide to behavior; Accepting one's physique; Achieving emotional independence of parents and other adults	Continuing spiritual development	Continuing personal and spiritual growth; (If married) Assisting teenage children to become responsible adults	Continuing spiritual development; Developing new recreational interests; Making a conscious effort to maintain one's physical and psychological flexibility
Environmental	Forming simple concepts of physical reality; Learning to walk; Learning to take solid foods; Learning to control the elimination of body wastes; (Achieving physiologi-...)	Developing concepts necessary for everyday living	Achieving assurance of economic independence; Selecting and preparing for an occupation; Using the body effectively	Getting established in an occupation; (If single) Establishing a way of living as a single person	Continuing to carry full responsibility in one's occupation; Accomplishing and adjusting to biological changes of middle age	Preparing for retirement from one's occupation and for reduced income; Establishing suitable living conditions; Adjusting to declining strength

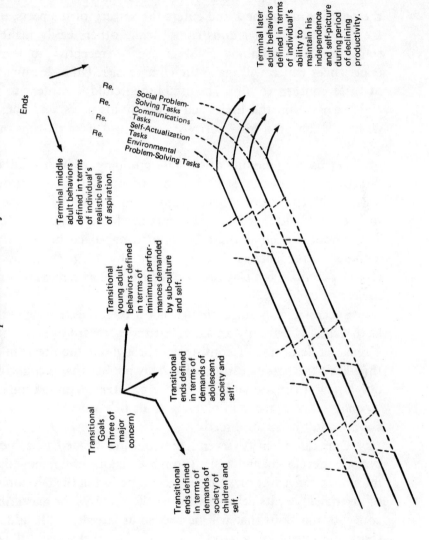

Figure 2

*Educational Pathways to Nurture
Developmental Task Performance*

Ends

Terminal middle
adult behaviors
defined in terms
of individual's
realistic level
of aspiration.

Re.
Re.
Re.
Re.

Social Problem-
Solving Tasks
Communications
Tasks
Self-Actualization
Tasks
Environmental
Problem-Solving Tasks

Terminal later
adult behaviors
defined in terms
of individual's
ability to
maintain his
independence
and self-picture
during period
of declining
productivity.

Transitional
young adult
behaviors defined
in terms of
minimum perfor-
mances demanded
by sub-culture
and self.

Transitional
Goals
(Three of
major
concern)

Transitional
ends defined
in terms of
demands of
adolescent
society and
self.

Transitional
ends defined
in terms of
demands of
society of
children and
self.

As a child enters into a formal education program, he is faced with several ascents and rests on several ledges which are quite clearly defined by the society. The five- or six-year-old child leaves the security of the nest and enters the society of his peers. Some are faced with a hazardous climb, while others easily make the transition. The climbing child is usually receptive to learning experiences which will make the climb easier. Other learnings are of little concern to him. The established child is content to play and learn within the limits laid down by his peers, and does not wish to climb until his security is threatened if he remains in the group.

Let us examine one of the task groupings of later childhood, "building wholesome attitudes toward one's self as a growing organism." The tasks contain many elements belonging uniquely to later childhood, and also elements needed at subsequent levels. For instance, a child must be able to approach his peers with confidence, recognizing that he has the physiological and psychological potential for playing an effective role as a member of the society of children.

Success at this stage, though not a prerequisite to success at later stages, is certainly an asset. Attitudes toward one's self show a remarkable degree of consistency throughout the life span, and they have their roots early in life. This implies that a concern for developing a functional behavior during later childhood might be far more advantageous in building adult behaviors than "teaching about" adult behavior directly.

One can identify several prerequisites needed to achieve a period's developmental task. Though a major developmental task must be achieved at or about a certain period in the development of an individual, its achievement usually involves the mastering of concepts and skills that will be needed at later levels. In addition, the achievement of a task at a particular level usually depends upon successful achievement of certain prerequisite tasks at an earlier period. This means that an efficient, effective developmental-task-oriented educational program cannot be concerned solely with life adjustment problems at a particular moment, but must also concern itself with the scope and sequence charts which have so long plagued the traditionalists.

Returning to our "sweeping" analogy, the teacher has two major concerns as he clears the way for the learner. When the learner is struggling to ascend the maturation ladder, he needs help in selecting experiences which will aid him in achieving his major goals. When the learner is comfortably resting on a developmental plateau, he is likely to be more concerned with exploratory, creative, and appreciative activities, which are compatible with the standards of the group to which he belongs. If we were to let our criteria for weeding out inappropriate learning experiences be guided by the natural interests of the learner, we would have a satisfactory program for the developing of a happy "mass man," or "mass adolescent." If, however, we wish to concern ourselves with the development of responsible citizens capable of managing a complex technocracy and of improving the condition of man, we must sometimes sweep cracker crumbs into comfortable beds and must always keep the paths open to both the next security station and adulthood.

In the 1970s many of our schools are still essentially baby-sitting services, where the most effective acculturation activities take place during the *unsupervised* portions of the day. The term "wasteland" can be justifiably applied in many cases, because a monumental opportunity is being missed by the administrators of these institutions. The typical child in the United States is enrolled in elementary and secondary schools for about 2400 days. If the combined knowledge and skills of the psychologist, the sociologist, the criminologist, the anthropologist, and the educator were effectively used during these 2400 days, we should certainly move a long way toward the development of a self-actualizing, contributing citizenry.

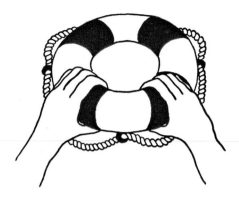

CHAPTER TWO

AN INSTRUCTIONAL LIFELINE:
GLOBAL BEHAVIORAL OBJECTIVES

A textbook with a supplementary student study guide has been providing teachers, students, administrators, and school boards a secure handrail for chaining together school experiences for more than a century. Yesterday, today, and tomorrow are rationally and materially joined with a continuity that is hard to duplicate. The people involved need this continuity, and although they are feeling increasingly guilty over the meaninglessness of many of the "learning activities," they see no alternative structures which could be substituted.

There *are* others, but they seem attractive only to those within a narrow range of talents and temperaments. For example:

Some teachers can live with a program based upon isolated activities which captivate and hold the interest of the child. They argue that an active, involved, thinking child is learning. The fact that he is involved and thinking indicates that learning is focused on his interests and his needs at an appropriate developmental level. The teacher is therefore secure in the notion that as long as he can provide learner-involving activities, he is doing his job.

Some teachers focus on the teaching of process skills, such as critical thinking, experimenting, hypothesizing, predicting, observing, etc. Any "learning activity" which either nurtures such skills or *should* nurture such skills can be built into the program with confidence.

Some teachers feel that attitudes or appreciations are all-important. A teacher can read poetry or play music to a class by the hour, radiating his enthusiasm for the beauty of the words or music, assured that this enthusiasm will transfer to the learner—thus justifying all his efforts.

Some teachers operating within such orientations often do produce remarkable behavioral changes. But must we rely on trusting that these behavioral changes will occur through the application of broad, general instructional strategies in shotgun fashion? Or can specific behavior be defined and developed in a *systematic* way, changing the teacher's role and "lifeline" from a text discusser, a workbook drillmaster, or an activity organizer to a behavior changer? The evidence of educational technology and behavioral psychology supports the feasibility of the behaviorally oriented instructional movement.

Chapter One suggested a dream role for tomorrow's schools, where the graduating student:

1. successfully meets his needs by solving the social and physical environmental problems with which he is confronted,
2. confidently and self-assuredly faces successive problems,
3. behaves in such a manner as to enhance the self-actualization of those falling under the influence of his actions.

When we look at our schools and then at our dream, most of us feel like the child who was asked directions to a familiar place, but one which was not tied in any way to the site of the inquiry. Her response was, "You can't get there from here."

Our teachers are traditionally oriented to passing on discipline-based knowledge through a lock-step textbook medium. And you *can't* get there directly from here. The textbook and the discipline are a security blanket for both the teachers and the students. One cannot take it away without an extensive re-education program and the substitution of *another* security blanket.

In this chapter we will examine the "behavioral objectives movement" to determine its relevance in making our schools more effective in nurturing happy, contributing, problem-solving citizens. Let's look at the movement, some divergent paths its adherents are taking, and some of the ways in which it can be used to improve our schools.

The Behavioral Objectives Movement

The twentieth century, with its Ivan Pavlovs, E.L. Thorndikes, J.B. Watsons, and B.F. Skinners, has witnessed a concerted, continuous effort to make a *science* of the education process. The movement attempts to explain complex learning in terms of a systematic chaining of minute bits of conditioned behaviors. The purpose of the quest is to develop learning systems that will efficiently produce desired behaviors.

"Behavioral psychology," "behavioral technology," "programmed instruction," and "systems technology" are labels of the movement which became part of every intellectual's vocabulary in the 1960s. The major concern has been to program learning, and the first step in the process is to *define the learning desired.*

Learning is defined by the psychologist as a change in behavior resulting from experience. Programming instruction requires, therefore, that the desired behavior be defined precisely, and broken down into teachable components which can be chained together to produce the desired performance.

The late 50s and early 60s produced a wave of individualized, programmed instructional materials following the educational technologists' guidelines. Pieces of these materials could be found in schools throughout the nation. Mathematics, grammar, and geography skills were favorite foci, because the content was logically ordered and sequenced, and energetic teachers in these fields, armed with the right formulae, could quickly produce the programs Most of the programs produced during this period were made by classroom teachers, were published without careful field testing, and were generally of poor quality. The result was that the wave was dissipated and the wave riders were disillusioned.

The behavioral objective concept is quite easily communicated but, as we shall later see, the teaching of skills for implementation is considerably more difficult.

A behavioral objective is simply a statement regarding the behavior expected of a learner as a result of an instructional sequence Six characteristics of an appropriately stated objective are

1. It describes the behavior expected.
2. It describes the behavior in detail.
3. It describes the conditions under which the behavior will be performed.
4. It is a realistic objective for the learner.
5. The behavior can be observed.
6. The quality of the performance can be evaluated.

For a century the American public schools have committed themselves to "book learning." Few teachers could describe the functional behaviors their lessons were supposed to nurture—e.g., reading *Silas Marner*, conjugating verbs, finding square roots, or studying the geography of Afghanistan. Now that the home, school, and neighborhood are relinquishing their training roles, the school must re-evaluate its role, establishing new priorities. The goals which should be given top priorities are certainly the behaviors needed to solve daily problems related to the social world, the physical world, and the inner world of the self. The schools can afford to entertain children and cater to their whims only after they provide for the development of the priority behaviors.

The behavioral objective is not only valid in identifying objectives for classroom instruction, but is equally valid for modifying behavior on the school bus, on the playground, in the locker room, etc., thereby bringing the whole school curriculum under rational guidance.

Orientations to the
Use of Behavioral Objectives

In this section the reader is asked to make some discriminations which many of the "experts" have *not* made. There is *not* a single, unified movement in education pushing for behavioral objectives—there are many, and they are often at odds with each other. Figure 3 identifies eight such perspectives, although a competent teacher might be able to assume several of these.

Three categories of educators are identified in the left-hand column. The first is the designer and/or writer of individualized programs for publication. He is typically an orderly, systematic worker, striving for an efficient instructional package. His product is seldom field tested until it has been written, and so it is held together not by empirically validated elements, but by the logic of the creator. Most vocal contemporary advocates of behavior-based instruction perceive the task from the programmer's point of view.

The second category of educators involved in the behavioral objectives movement is the conscientious, professional, classroom teacher, who recognizes that if the classroom is to be more than a grouping unit for "baby sitting," the teacher must be able to identify the behavioral objective appropriate to the needs of the learner and guide the individual learner toward the achievement of the behaviors. The teacher, unlike the programmer, is confronted with reality daily; he cannot afford the luxury of a purely *logical* instructional system. Left to his ingenuity, the teacher can improvise motivational systems, reinforcement schedules, and instructional experiences which the programmer cannot. The

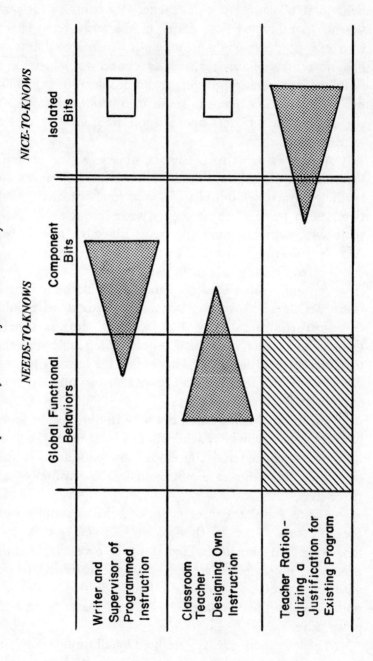

Figure 3

Perspectives for Use of Behavioral Objectives

behavioral objective to this teacher is a compass for planning—yearly, monthly, weekly, daily, momentarily, etc. The teacher who can sit down with a student to help him define a set of behaviors that he can realistically expect to achieve in writing legibility, computation power, group problem-solving ability, etc., has an orientation that can result in functional learning and free the teacher to rely less and less on traditional staples such as lecture and textbook.

A third category of behavioral objective users includes those who feel they should use them because their colleagues do. Their teaching format seldom changes as a result of their new "objective." Such teachers might simply wade through their lectures or textbooks, writing a knowledge-recall objective for each page. The text is still the focus of instruction—the teacher has simply constructed a battery of *test items.*

Certainly, some teachers can and should be writing instructional packages for others. They will require extensive skills in the first instructional category. Far more teachers can benefit from the second orientation, which is quite compatible with that used in "behavior modification." The teacher is a learning manager who can identify the learner's objectives and can plan experiences to appropriately modify behaviors.

The third orientation is not very useful; it contributes little to functional learning. Teachers in this category might be assigned objectives and materials developed by educators in the other categories, but they are not actually "behaviorally oriented" themselves.

Figure 3 isolates three types of behavioral objectives across the top row. First is the global behavior, which is usually long-range and can be broken down into teachable component behaviors. Both the programmer and the analytical teacher deal with objectives of this kind. Those dealing with behavioral objectives at the "isolated bits" level have no use for this perspective.

The "component bits" are used by all three groups and focus

on "needs-to-know" behaviors. The programmer and analytical teacher derive the "needs-to-know" objectives from the global behaviors. At the isolated bit level, however, the teacher arbitrarily declares them "needed."

The "nice-to-knows" in the "isolated bits" column contain the transitional behaviors (those needed at the early stages of instruction but which atrophy when the global behavior is reached) as well as the niceties that are cherished by the teacher but have little to do with the global behavior. Few teachers and perhaps even fewer programmers can refrain from including many of these in their instructional programs. "Needs-to-know" objectives should certainly be given priority, and instruction which is heavily weighted on the "nice-to-know" side requires modification. The ideal ratio of "nice-to-know" to "needs-to-know" objectives in teacher-managed instruction can't be specified—but it should certainly be closer to "0" than "1."

The two upper triangles appearing in Figure 3 identify, by their area, an emphasis in two productive behavioral objective thrusts. When the individual concerned is writing a program for publication, he analyzes the global behavior once and then concentrates on the bits derived. The teacher, however, will find the global objective the more useful tool. It provides a manageable number of objectives for the teacher to monitor and allows freedom for the teacher to break the objective down into different components for individualizing instruction.

The four instructional maps appearing in Part II of this book identify a "starter set" of global objectives for a problem-centered curriculum in general education. The maps are well enough organized so that a professional educator could learn to "conjure them up," without assistance, in a few hours. A school staff—so oriented—could speak a common language regarding the nature of, and identify priorities for, their concerns.

Global behavioral objectives derived from these maps can serve teachers with a wide variety of teaching and life styles. While the atomized objectives used by the programmer "turn off" all but the highly analytical and the new conformist, the global approach has room for all. The analytical teacher can break the global behaviors into a number of components appropriate to his instructional competencies and styles, while the non-analytical teacher can purchase programs developing these behaviors, or he can generate activities that will nurture such behaviors.

Teacher educators have erred in their behavioral objective thrust. Teachers must focus on behavioral change, but their major thrust should be on global functional behaviors. This book is an attempt to provide such a thrust. The child citizen is a problem-solver, living in social, communications, self-actualizing and physical-environmental worlds. These worlds can be broken down into global functional behaviors which will serve as the teacher's *instructional handles.*

Consider the following objective: the typical, healthy, fourth grade boy should catch half the fly balls that come to him in the outfield, prevent a base runner from advancing more than one base after he (the fielder) touches the ball, and maintain a .250 batting average when playing with age peers.

Typical programmed instruction approaches to the objective could follow two routes:

1. A single, linear programmed route where the objective would be analyzed into many sub-behaviors, and learning experiences would be created and chained into a series of programmed exercises for all, or

2. A two-faceted program where
    a. the learner would be assigned to a peer-group ball team where play would be regularly scheduled, and

    b. the learner's behavior would be analyzed in terms of the global objectives, and special mini-remedial programs would be called upon to polish the behavior to the criterion defined in the objective.

The latter approach is probably more effective, where either mini-remedial programs or sufficient tutors are available.

The former approach is possibly more effective where no competent instructor or very few learners are available.

Now, perhaps, we should rethink the role of the objective in the learning process. In Skinner's classic experiments with the dancing pigeon, a teaching machine was built and the pigeon trained to peck at a disc in the "box" when a buzzer was sounded, causing a food reinforcement to appear. The bird was then placed in the Skinner box for the dancing lesson. The initial task was to get the bird to make two complete turns to the right. To do this, every time the hungry pigeon turned slightly to the right the buzzer was sounded, it pecked the disc, and it was rewarded. When the bird consistently turned a quarter turn to the right, reinforcement stopped until he moved (say) a 3/8 turn to the right. The process was continued until the subject moved consistently.

In the classroom we can speed up portions of the process through verbal mediation so that the child can make the double turn on the first trial, although the sequencing of several steps into a smoothly executed dance routine would require a reinforcement program quite similar to that used on the pigeon. The reader is cautioned that he is not being asked to equate the training of pigeons with the educating of children. Man's verbal mediation system adds dimensions which complicate the process. Both learning situations, however, require the following instructional planning:

1.   Identification of global behaviors desired.
2.   Identification of rewards that will reinforce learner behavior.
3.   Analysis of global behaviors into component teachable behaviors.
4.   A sequence of appropriate learning experiences to nurture the desired behaviors, where successive improved performances are reinforced.

Let us now look to another developmental concern dealing with nutrition and eating habits. The three behavioral objectives listed below focus on three classical approaches to instruction—a knowledge approach, a skill approach, and a functional behavior approach.

1. The learner will describe the six basic nutritional needs of the body and the foods that will satisfy these needs (knowledge).
2. The learner will use a calorie chart to calculate, within 15 percent, the calories of meals pictured on serving trays (skill).
3. The learner will maintain appropriate body weight, blood cholesterol count, and blood sugar count norms, using charts prepared by school physicians and results from annual physical examinations and monthly weight checks (functional).

Certainly the knowledge approach is the *easiest* one to handle. We know, however, that it will be effective in changing functional behaviors only in the very bright and/or strongly inner-directed individual. The skill approach requires considerably more effort to manage and deals with the systematic building of isolated skills which the individual could use in monitoring his nutritional intake. It usually fails, because it does not develop the attitudes necessary to trigger the application of the skill when the need for it arises. The third approach, however, uses the learner's world as a Skinner box, where appropriate learner decisions at breakfast, in the cafeteria, or between meals require monitoring with appropriate reinforcements.

Viewing the *child's world as a Skinner box or a learning laboratory* which needs monitoring and reinforcing by the teacher is a bold notion. Certainly, comprehensive monitoring will never be possible. However, by simulating life-like conditions in the classroom, enlisting the cooperation of out-of-class resources (such as the family) to reinforce behaviors, and viewing the child's school world as more than the classroom (in this case the cafeteria might be perceived as a Skinner box for nurturing appropriate eating habits), the sterile classroom can be brought to life.

The above diagram portrays the child's real world in terms of his physique and his cafeteria selections. His actual selections are dependent upon the strengths of his attitudes toward the particular foods and the knowledge and skills he has acquired. An effective functional instructional program must be, first and foremost, grounded in the real world. Its component parts, however, include knowledge and skills together with the attitudes that will precipitate them.

In this chapter we have explored the notion that a series of global behavioral objectives can provide the educator and the learner with a secure lifeline around which instructional experiences can be built. However, unlike the traditional textbook, this orientation leads to functional, life-serving behaviors. Chapter Three will explore the role of the subject matter disciplines in the process of weaning the educator from the text to the behavioral lifeline.

CHAPTER THREE

BEHAVIORAL OBJECTIVES AND THE
ACADEMIC DISCIPLINES

The academic disciplines currently provide the glue for rational and orderly day-to-day confrontations between teacher and pupil. They give the uninvolved or disoriented teacher a perspective for planning future sessions and evaluating past performances. The dominant place of skill development in the primary grades progressively and quickly gives way to the disciplines as the rudiments are achieved and the sophisticated pre-adolescent begins to rebel against a busy-work curriculum.

Few elementary or junior high school teachers, however, would argue that an educated adolescent will emerge when the child masters the prescribed disciplines. The task of teachers is to keep an eye on the behaviors exhibited in their classrooms and adapt the instruction to meet the needs indicated. The alert, sensitive teacher who can depart from the discipline to minister to an individual's needs makes a school curriculum vital.

The core courses of our curricula have not changed appreciably in over 2000 years. The Romans, with their grammar-rhetoric concerns, dialectic-ethic concerns, arithmetic-geometry concerns, astronomy concerns, and music concerns, had a curriculum remarkably similar to ours, with its English, social studies, mathematics, science, and fine arts. Although these areas periodically become impoverished and sterile (as in the Dark Ages or even in pre-Sputnik U.S.), rumblings occur and revisions are made so that a semblance of vitality is restored. What is there about these disciplines that makes them prevail?

The writer maintains that this question can be easily answered if we consider the task of education as that of making problem-solvers out of our youth. The child who can solve his problems in each of the following areas has the prerequisites for sustaining both his own self-fulfilled existence and also a free and supportive society:

1. Problems with people and social institutions.
2. Problems with communications.
3. Problems with his aesthetic world and his self-actualization.
4. Problems with his physical environment.

Although these domains are not mutually exclusive, they identify the predominant clusters of problems which have confronted Western man since antiquity. It is certainly not a coincidence that knowledge has tended to be organized in packages following the same cluster patterns. The clusters seem to have a grass-roots base. This means that a curriculum path can begin in the early childhood years around clusters of rudimentary practical skills (language, social, etc.) and emerge with a similar cluster capable of shaping pioneer thinkers who can push back the frontiers of knowledge.

The central curricular problem, however, is that the disciplines deal with abstractions, while most young children and many older children find it difficult—if not impossible—to translate the abstractions into functional problem-solving tools. Dividing fractions, diagramming sentences, balancing chemical equations, charting political systems, comparing musical or painting styles, etc., are but a few examples. Even those who are proficient in manipulating abstractions often find it impossible to jump the barrier to *reality*. Thus the discipline provides the teacher-pupil-classroom complex with abstract knowledge which must be converted to a child's perspective to become meaningful and useful.

The teacher's task is to appraise the child's problem-solving ability in each of the areas mentioned above and to coordinate appropriate learning experiences so that the child will become more proficient in his problem-solving. This means concocting the right mix of simulated, concrete experiences and discipline-related abstract conceptualizations so that learning is functional and efficient.

The following diagram (Figure 4) shows the four basic problem-solving areas of the learner, the disciplines related to the needs, and the task of the teacher in structuring appropriate learning experiences. (The term "problem-solving" does not imply a single set of "problem-solving" skills. It simply implies that the adaptive learner must develop a variety of skills in a variety of areas which will facilitate his attempts to satisfy his needs. Each of these areas might require several separate sets of problem-solving abilities.)

The cone in the diagram is divided into four gores, each representing a developmental area:

1. *The Social Problems Area*: Here the child is viewed as a social being, trying to establish satisfying social relationships with both peers and adults. While the *child* usually considers this task of prime importance, the *curriculum* tends instead to emphasize historical and social science bodies of knowledge.

2. *The Communications Problems Area*: Although communications could be classified as social, the traditional curriculum pattern and teaching specialties justify separate consideration. At an early age the child must communicate to others his felt needs, and must support his peers and family members as they struggle to

Figure 4

*Behavioral Objectives and the Disciplines
in General Education*

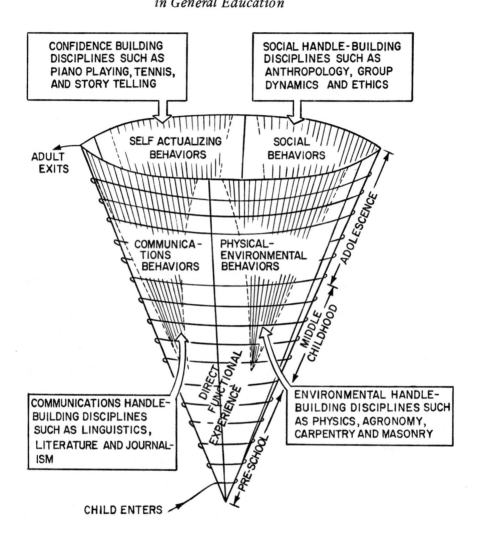

realize their physical and social needs. Reading and writing are two communications tasks given a high priority in the school. Oral communication and listening skills, however, are often neglected.

3. *The Self-Actualization Problems Area*: Ideally the individual, in his hourly encounters with life's problems, should maintain a positive attitude toward himself, his talents, and his abilities, and a confidence that he is up to the challenges tomorrow will bring. Self-Actualization is listed as a problem area because the individual can identify moments when his opinion of himself is deteriorating, and can move to engage in activities that will remedy the situation. Everyone can become skilled in activities and creative media where his abilities can be recognized. However, identifying these strengths and providing the opportunity to develop the needed skills are difficult tasks. A competent teacher offering considerable guidance is required to help each child acquire his own unique package. Self-actualization is nurtured by chains of successes in the other problem-solving areas as well as in activities existing primarily for "re-creation."

4. *The Environmental Problems Area*: The child who cannot solve problems in his physical world and make his physical world work for him is likely to live a life of frustration. He is expected to solve problems related to keeping things clean, moving heavy weights, nurturing plant and animal life, repairing broken toys, and performing a host of other tasks related to his environment. Science and mathematics classes deal with these problems in the abstract, but typically only the academically oriented benefit from such instruction.

The point of the cone in the diagram represents the individual at birth, when his experiences are nil. The circling spiral indicates the individual as he encounters experiences in each of the problem areas during his maturation. During the pre-school years, most homes provide many opportunities in each area for the child to meet and overcome problems with the help of parents and siblings. The cone further suggests that this should be the structure of the elementary and secondary schools. As the individual becomes more mature, and more is expected of him, he will need more sophisticated solutions to the problems in each area. The school should help him to contrive the appropriate solutions.

The shaded triangles in each of the four areas represent the traditional disciplines, with their bodies of knowledge and skills. As the child enters the upper elementary grades, he begins to encounter formal studies in these disciplines. The social area is concerned with the social sciences, psychology, economic geography, and the like. The communications area deals with reading, writing, composition, listening, and speaking, as well as analyzing communications and organizing persuasive arguments. The self-realization area taps the fields of psychology, art, music, philosophy, religion, and history. The environmental area includes disciplines in the physical and natural sciences, public health, and vocations. Because the categories overlap, some disciplines may fit well into more than one area.

Let us now look for a moment at the faces below:

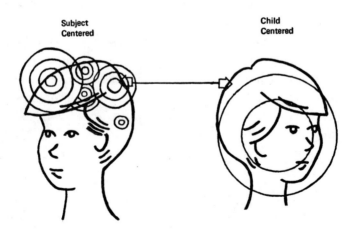

Subject
Centered

Child
Centered

The child at the left portrays a learning pattern typical of a pupil in an extremely subject-oriented instructional setting, while the child at the right epitomizes a learner in a child-centered pattern. One hundred years ago the prevailing psychology of the classroom was called "faculty psychology." It assumed that the brain was organized into a number of specialized centers, each of which needed nurturing if the individual were to function at capacity. These centers included a memory center, a numbers center, a musical center, and a reasoning center, among others. The pseudo-science of phrenology, stemming from a similar orientation, assumes that one's abilities and future can be ascertained by reading the bumps on the head. Many of the subjects imbedded in today's curriculum were justified because they were thought to nurture one or more of the faculties. This orientation supposes that a learner should be subjected to a variety of unrelated disciplines, each promoting development of a faculty. Gradually the concerns of the faculties broaden until they overlap, and an individual emerges who has a functional, rational control of the primary elements of his environment.

Contrast his outlook with the orientation of the child-centered learner. His educational experiences are selected because they focus upon his real, immediate problems. When he has an unanswered question—probably related to one of the four areas in the cone—this becomes his focus until it is solved. Therefore the individual's learning is not fragmented, and he tends to be an integrated individual throughout the whole learning process.

Looking back to the cone, we find that early childhood and most of middle childhood stress the child-centered developmental approach, while the adolescent period shifts its emphasis to a predominantly subject-centered approach. The typical child in the discipline-based curriculum reacts as if he were being immersed in one discipline after another, with a few minutes' breather in between. Many of these children are set adrift—or drowned—in a succession of disciplines throughout the day. It is apparent to the romantic that the child-based rather than the discipline-based curriculum is the more attractive. The more experienced and the less imaginative teachers tend to avoid it, because it is most difficult to manage. *Both* the humanist-artist-teacher and the behavioral technologist-teacher have Utopian dreams of a functional child-centered curriculum. Unfortunately, neither one has charted the system, nor can collect the materials necessary to make the task a viable one in the near future—certainly not one which the average teacher can manage in a 40- to 50-hour week. The child, too, is rebelling against the meaninglessness of the discipline-centered game, yet at the same time is frightened by the disorder of the child-centered classroom tenuously held together only by the personality of the teacher.

A viable structure for the mainstream school curriculum of the 1970s is one guided by a cognitive, discipline-based thread, yet geared to making the child's social, communication, self-actualization, and physical-environmental problem-solving world more intelligible to him. The 1980s might find teachers weaned from this discipline base. By then behavioral objectives, with accompanying individualized instructional packages, should be readily available, with a management system that can provide adequate security for all participants.

The Role of the Academic Disciplines in the 1970s

Not many educators aware of the magnitude of the behavioral, technological, and humanistic movements shaking the foundations of our educational structures would wager that the traditional disciplines will emerge unscathed. If these dissenting groups had recognized the magnitude of their task or the inertia of their foe, they might never have initiated their attack. The thrust, however, has begun, and the industrial complex is tooled for production, but the assembly line is moving slowly.

Two obvious barriers to change will not be overcome for at

least a decade. First, comprehensive, modular instructional materials have not been produced. Second, the instructional staffs of the nation's educational institutions have neither the skills nor the inclination to build and man such systems.

We desperately need a discipline-based curriculum for the 1970s that explores human experience—social, communicative, self-actualizing, and environmental (survival). Such a curriculum can provide the teacher with the stability and system he needs, and the curriculum maker with a base for developing functional packages to tie the concepts to the learner's world. While the materials are being developed, the teacher, with his professional skills and insights, serves as the prime mover in the development of functional problem-solving skills. As materials are developed, the teacher's concerns will become more sophisticated, for he will be able to focus his attention on the individual learner.

Today the educational world is not ready to "go systems," yet neither is the systems world. The humanist movement, too, needs to clarify many of its concepts before attempting to implement them.

A truce period is needed, where teachers, behaviorists, and humanists can agree to use for a time a modification of a contemporary, quasi-discipline-based curriculum. Such a curriculum should be compatible with the desires of all three approaches yet capable, today, of captivating the student—in transition—with his "bag." Courses developed through the High School Geography Project at the University of Colorado (1969) or the Taba Curriculum Development Project at San Francisco State College (1965) or the Social Studies Curriculum Program (particularly *Man: A Course of Study,* 1970) at the Education Development Center at Cambridge, Massachusetts, might serve as examples in the social sphere. (See Sanders, 1970.) In the math-science area the American Association for the Advancement of Science's *Science: A Process Approach* (1968) might serve. (For a full description, see Cole, Henry P. *Process Education,* 1972.)

Although most teachers could adjust to this kind of

curricular change without loss of effectiveness, the notion of converting an academic discipline to a problem-solving, skill-building curriculum has not even occurred to many teachers. Extensive efforts in both pre-service and in-service instruction would be required to realize this goal.

The teacher must:

1. be able to view his discipline both from within and from without, and to acquire a similar perspective about related disciplines;

2. be able to perceive the discipline elements (knowledge, attitudes, and skills) as tools in problem-solving;

3. be able to identify the kinds of discipline-related problems the learner is likely to encounter in the near and distant future and to build appropriate bridges for transfer;

4. be able to view the discipline not only from the view of the expert, but also from the perspective of a young learner with only partial insights into its intricacies; and

5. be able to assist learners in building on their conception of the discipline so that it remains functional yet organized.

In the past, when society was stable and a parent could orient the learner to the problem-solving world, the post-primary school could afford the luxury of teaching "nice-to-knows" to a leisure class. We are now in a period of transition, where functional objectives must be given priorities, but where teacher competencies and styles must be considered in task assignments. Those that can keep order can do *that* until replacements can be obtained. Those that can teach the knowledge of a discipline can be encouraged to operate in a broader discipline, and to occasionally minister to the problem-solving needs of their learners. Those who have the drive and the perspective should have the option of departing from the discipline curriculum for extensive periods to make functional the knowledge that other, more restricted, teachers have imparted.

The Teacher and His Dream

The schoolmarm of the nineteenth century is gradually giving way to the professional educator, knowledgeable about child development and behavior-shaping strategies and about one or more disciplines. While the teacher of a century ago wanted a formula so that the job could be automated, today's teacher would like to play a greater role in making instruction functional and relevant to the learner.

However, the teacher who makes a beeline attack on the developing of functional behaviors usually emerges with a fragmented, chaotic program and a nervous breakdown. One cannot easily manage a classroom where one learner is learning to set a table, another talk on the telephone, and another analyze the causes of the Vietnam war. Mainstream programs are required which give direction and continuity to every child's program, yet provide points of departure for each learner to enrich his life by pursuing concepts which especially interest him.

Nearly all teachers can readily adapt to a change in textbook, so long as the knowledge base remains in his area of competency. A text which also concentrates on themes deemed relevant to the learner and knowledge useful to the learner would yield added bonuses.

A teacher unwilling to take on any new obligations could still be more effective with materials such as these. Chronological world history, chronological English literature, classical Euclidian geometry, and biological nomenclature are easy to surpass for theme relevance and problem-solving related knowledge.

The artist-teacher, too, can use suitable moments in such a text program as points of departure for creative activities suitable to individual learners.

Course materials today must suggest tunes that will make the learners dance. The teachers will have to rely on their ingenuity and resources to teach the basic skills until more comprehensive materials and techniques are developed. Neither a funeral dirge nor sophisticated Bach will serve as the musical themes, because they will fail to stimulate the learner into vital, disciplined activity. The prime mover in any dynamic classroom nurturing problem-solving skills is a teacher who can modulate freely across traditional subject matter lines and translate discipline-based skills and concepts so that they become functional problem-solving tools for the learner.

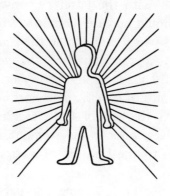

PART II

FOUR MAPS FOR CHARTING A
SCHOOL'S CURRICULUM

The term "general education" has been used for many years to define the focus of the elementary and junior high school. It implies a basic education needed by the young American to live in today's world. A century ago, when non-school institutions carried the major general education load, the school's primary concern was the "three R's." Today the family, church, and neighborhood have abandoned considerable portions of their general education functions, while the school has rather haphazardly taken on additional concerns. We are left, however, with a smorgasbord of content, activities, and objectives which we call a general education curriculum but which eludes definition.

Is the opposite of *general education* specific education or vocation-centered education? This is a crucial question, because its answer orients the curriculum maker and teacher in the elementary and junior high school to the criteria for the selection of objectives. If the answer to the question is "specific," then the vagueness of our current curriculum is justified. If the answer is "vocation-centered," then some soul searching is needed. The

writer aligns himself with the latter response and argues that a
general education should nurture specific social, manipulative, and
perceptual behaviors which will enable the learner to pull his own
weight in society and contribute to the general welfare in a
manner which is self-enhancing and satisfying. General education
refers to the developing of specific behaviors needed by citizens in
all walks of life. As the school child matures and narrows his
vocational perspectives, his curricular emphasis changes from the
training of a citizen to the training of a vocationally competent
citizen.

The diagrams on the following five pages (Figure 5 series)
provide the core of the message of this book. If a school's staff
could be persuaded to commit itself to the five interrelated
vantage points, interpersonal conflict regarding curricular decisions
could be minimized, while a unified directed thrust compatible
with the needs of learners and faculty could be attained. Figure 5a
(introduced in Chapter Three) portrays the growing child interact-
ing with his world in a series of social, communications,
self-actualizing, and environmental encounters. These encounters
can be viewed as opportunities for the child to get handles on the
perennial problems of his world. A vital school curriculum assists
the learner in monitoring his problem-solving behavior to improve
his effectiveness. Chapter Four charts the social world of the
learner (see Figure 5b) in the interpersonal and institutional
settings. Chapter Five (see Figure 5c) examines the communications world of the learner, with the skills, knowledge, and
attitudes needed to cope with it. Chapter Six explores the child's
self-actualizing world (see Figure 5d), in which he acquires a
self-assurance which will enable him both to cope with difficult
problems and to delight in the process. Finally, Chapter Seven
views the learner in a complex physical environment (see Figure
5e), suggesting the knowledge, skills, and attitudes required to
make this environment serve both himself and the larger society.

The author takes the position that every teacher and
curriculum maker (and possibly every learner) should be able to

Figure 5a

Behavioral Objectives and the Disciplines in General Education

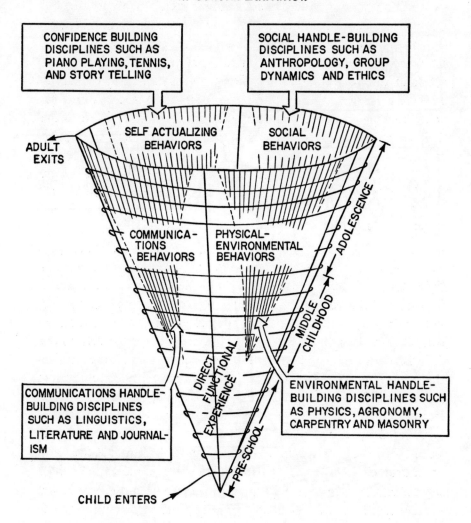

Figure 5b

The Social World of a Learner
in a Democracy

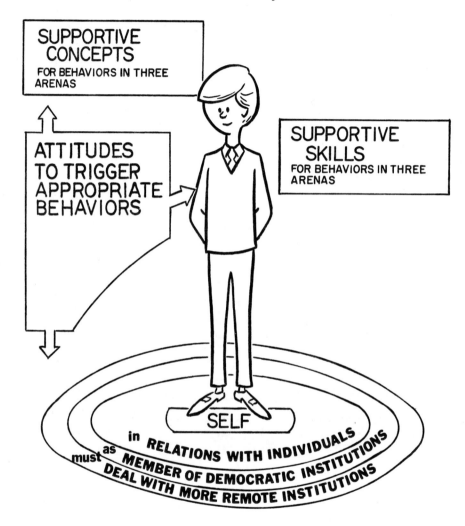

SUPPORTIVE
CONCEPTS
FOR BEHAVIORS IN THREE
ARENAS

ATTITUDES
TO TRIGGER
APPROPRIATE
BEHAVIORS

SUPPORTIVE
SKILLS
FOR BEHAVIORS IN THREE
ARENAS

SELF

in RELATIONS WITH INDIVIDUALS
must as MEMBER OF DEMOCRATIC INSTITUTIONS
DEAL WITH MORE REMOTE INSTITUTIONS

Figure 5c

The Learner's Communications World

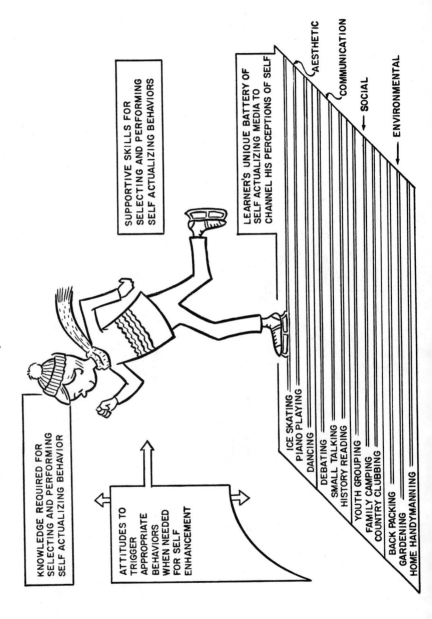

Figure 5d

The Self-Actualizing World
of the Learner

SUPPORTIVE SKILLS FOR SELECTING AND PERFORMING SELF ACTUALIZING BEHAVIORS

LEARNER'S UNIQUE BATTERY OF SELF ACTUALIZING MEDIA TO CHANNEL HIS PERCEPTIONS OF SELF

AESTHETIC

COMMUNICATION

SOCIAL

ENVIRONMENTAL

KNOWLEDGE REQUIRED FOR SELECTING AND PERFORMING SELF ACTUALIZING BEHAVIOR

ATTITUDES TO TRIGGER APPROPRIATE BEHAVIORS WHEN NEEDED FOR SELF ENHANCEMENT

ICE SKATING
PIANO PLAYING
DANCING

DEBATING
SMALL TALKING
HISTORY READING

YOUTH GROUPING
FAMILY CAMPING
COUNTRY CLUBBING

BACK PACKING
GARDENING
HOME HANDYMANNING

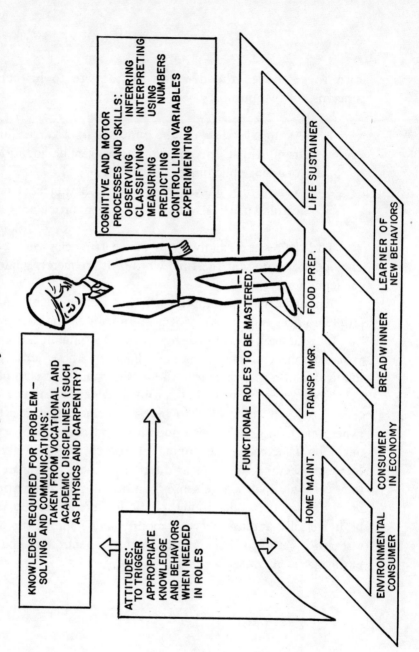

Figure 5e

Objectives Concerned with
Harnessing One's Physical Environment

KNOWLEDGE REQUIRED FOR PROBLEM –
SOLVING AND COMMUNICATIONS:
TAKEN FROM VOCATIONAL AND
ACADEMIC DISCIPLINES (SUCH
AS PHYSICS AND CARPENTRY)

COGNITIVE AND MOTOR
PROCESSES AND SKILLS:
OBSERVING   INFERRING
CLASSIFYING   INTERPRETING
MEASURING   USING
PREDICTING   NUMBERS
CONTROLLING VARIABLES
EXPERIMENTING

ATTITUDES:
TO TRIGGER
APPROPRIATE
KNOWLEDGE
AND BEHAVIORS
WHEN NEEDED
IN ROLES

FUNCTIONAL ROLES TO BE MASTERED:

HOME MAINT.   TRANSP. MGR.   FOOD PREP.   LIFE SUSTAINER

ENVIRONMENTAL   CONSUMER   BREADWINNER   LEARNER OF
CONSUMER   IN ECONOMY   NEW BEHAVIORS

learn to reproduce the diagrams appropriate to his curricular concerns, for two purposes:

1.   As an overview of the function of a curriculum area from which specific objectives can be identified for long-range planning.
2.   As a device for evaluating a particular objective or set of learning materials for use in a larger curriculum.

The figures are simply maps for charting curricular courses. They do not represent the final word, but are merely guides for a curriculum in transition.

An underlying assumption of this section is that man is a problem-solver and that most of his problems can be classified into the four domains explored here—social, communications, self-actualization, and environmental. Each of these areas is then subdivided into role categories the learner typically has to play.

Research indicates that problem-solving is not a broad, generalized skill, but tends to be compartmentalized, so that an expert mechanic might be a poor husband and a poor gardener might be an excellent accountant. Research alone can determine the legitimacy of the roles as discrete problem-solving areas, but they certainly make more sense than our current assumption that skills like inferring, classifying, predicting, etc., once learned, can be universally applied. We can modify and improve the maps as research is gathered. Let us consider this as a *starter set* to be used in the classroom *today*.

CHAPTER FOUR

BEHAVIORAL OBJECTIVES FOR THE
SOCIAL STUDIES IN GENERAL EDUCATION

Every school district in the nation has at one time or another pledged its allegiance to a written collection of social studies objectives. Some of these statements emphasize mastery of an academic discipline, while others focus on the development of a public-spirited citizen. Nevertheless, nearly all the objectives are phrased in terms of intellectual concept development rather than specific interpersonal or individual-institutional behaviors.

In its *Handbook for Social Studies,* the Association of Teachers of Social Studies of the City of New York (1967) specifies the following purposes:

Experience in Cooperation
Appreciation of the Cultural Heritage
Intellectual Curiosity and Critical-Mindedness
Respect for Accuracy and Suspended Judgment
Intellectual Humility and Tolerance
Ability to Think Clearly
Love of History and Allied Subjects

These objectives are a mixture of attitudes, experiences, and psychological states. No terminal behaviors are defined, and their vagueness makes it unlikely that any educator will attempt to flesh them out.

The Civic Education Project sponsored by the National Council for the Social Studies (Roselle, 1966) defines its objectives in terms of twelve citizenship goals for a new age. The first two call for development of "a citizen who believes in both liberty of the individual and equality of rights for all, as provided by the Constitution of the United States," and "a citizen who recognizes that we live in an 'open end' world, and is receptive to new facts, new ideas, and new processes of living." The twelve goals emphasize intellectual constructs which are easy to evaluate with well-constructed essay questions yet bypass the overt citizen-related behaviors required for *living.*

A task force committee of the National Council for the Social Studies (1962) classifies its concerns under four headings—the behavioral needs in a free society, the beliefs of a free people, the role of knowledge, and the role of abilities and skills. This package contains the germ of a behaviorally oriented curricular base. It falls short, however, because the whole focus is on the making of an adult citizen. When the seventh grade teacher finds that she cannot evaluate the child's behavior by adult standards, she reverts to the academic objectives she can evaluate with a paper-and-pencil test. The learner soon recognizes that the only performances which *really count* in her classroom are those on the written examinations.

This writer believes that the chief objective of public school social studies is the development of specific social behaviors. These behaviors should enable the learner (1) to engage in mutually satisfying interpersonal relationships with members of his peer group and the larger society, (2) to participate actively and effectively in the life of his culture's institutions, acting to change institutions not meeting needs, and (3) to deal effectively as an institutional member in negotiating changes in other social institutions so that orderly social processes are maintained and the lives of the members of these institutions are enhanced.

Figure 6 should help us to explore these global concerns in more detail. The self-centered young learner lives in three social worlds. The innermost circle, and the one which is of the most pressing concern to him, is intimately related to the individuals he meets daily—his peers, his parents, his teachers, young children, and older children. As the child grows from infancy to adulthood, adult authority figures diminish in importance, and peers come to occupy more important roles. The learner's social world is therefore unstable; and, as he matures, he must learn different and more sophisticated behaviors. Schools, except for the primary grades, pay little attention to the development of behaviors in this area. When discipline problems arise, there is a concerted effort to remedy them, but this is not a major focus of the curriculum.

The second circle is concerned with the individual's social institutions. These include the family, the neighborhood, the school, a religious institution, peer groups, etc. Again, the family and the primary school make a token effort to acquaint the learner with community helpers, friends, neighbors, and the like. This emphasis is soon withdrawn, however, and the child is left to fend for himself. As in the case of interpersonal relationships, the democratic institutions to which the child belongs change as the child matures. The nursery school requires quite different behaviors than does the secondary school. The social relationship in the sandbox changes as the child progresses to the teen hangout or to the marijuana parties. A healthy social individual needs the support of our social institutions, modifying them when they become antiquated, but being careful to preserve those elements essential to a dynamic, supportive society.

The outermost circle is especially interesting, because it identifies the major focus of most of our social studies curricula. It is concerned with social institutions quite removed from the individual in his community. The individual can influence these remote institutions only through other institutions of which he is

Figure 6

The Social World of a Learner
in a Democracy

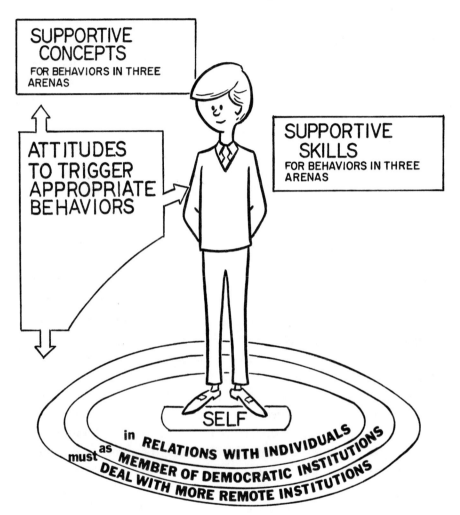

a member. He likely has few skills and insights and little power for exerting such influence. School children study the government of Pericles, life in the Roman Empire, the tribulations of the League of Nations, the Russian Revolution, etc. The concern is to give the individual a glimpse into the dynamics of sophisticated, historical, political, social, and economic institutions of yesterday and today. It is assumed that if one is aware of such events and can communicate adequately to his political representatives, he can bring about beneficial changes in the world scene. Hard evidence does not support this view.

It is not our mission here to deride any of these foci of concern. But it does seem appropriate to examine *priorities.* Our best-educated youths, fighting wars with foreign powers, and with remote elected representatives, seem hopelessly disillusioned. They appear to be unable to cope with the individuals about them and the social institutions with which they are affiliated. Our curriculum has its priorities reversed. Interpersonal relations with individuals seem to be the most pressing need of the individual, while we spend most of our class time on abstract, ethereal issues. In a sense we are fiddling while Rome burns.

The primary task of the social studies should be to provide the learner with the supportive concepts, skills, and attitudes that will enable him to cope with problems of his social world. He needs handles on his behaviors so that he can call upon them to solve his problems. When his friends avoid or attack him, he should be aware of his impulses and equipped with alternate behaviors that can remedy the situation. The school's curriculum should be organized to provide him with these handles. His major concern should be to master social skills concerned with conversing with others, problem-solving with others, helping others when they need it, etc. Many of these skills function automatically on the psychomotor level, but the individual needs supportive concepts which he can use to modify his behavior while he is engaged in these social activities. In addition, perhaps the most important single ingredient the learner requires is a set of attitudes which will alert him, and pressure him, to exhibit behaviors which will be truly problem-solving.

In this simple drawing (Figure 6) we have portrayed the learner's social predicament and the areas of concern important to the curriculum maker and the teacher as they guide learning experiences through the learner's formative years.

Few learners can derive functional behaviors from abstract academics. For these few we might justify a concentration in junior or senior high school on the academic side of history or the social sciences. For others, the direction and content of social studies should stress development of effective life-oriented and society-oriented behaviors.

A Further Breakdown of Objectives

The accompanying chart (Figure 7) of global objectives, although not exhaustive, goes a long way in specifying the behaviors essential to the learner in the 1970s. The four dimensions of concern overlap but, nevertheless, need individual attention. The first refers to the *global social behaviors* required for living in society. Second are *concepts* which a student might use to mediate social behaviors. Third are the intellectual and motor *skills* he needs to perform the behaviors. Fourth are the *attitudes* which trigger the performance of the behaviors. Although it might be possible to develop the global behaviors without some of the concepts and skills, we'll assume that the process is probably easier for most students if they have mastered a few core concepts and skills. The attitudes, though often neglected, are essential if the learned behaviors are ever to be recalled and used at an appropriate time.

The social world of the child is organized here under three headings: interpersonal relationships, relationships with his institutions, and relationships toward other institutions which result from his membership in his own institutions. If the social world of the child were to be viewed differently, the objectives might take another form, yet produce similar terminal behaviors.

The global behaviors related to interpersonal relationships are shown in the upper left corner of the chart. This section is concerned with encouraging the individual to take part in mutually rewarding relationships. Sometimes the student needs to acquire skill in playing games. Sometimes he needs new insights made possible by intellectual constructs. Both these tools can help to modify his behavior. Always, however, he must be committed to the behavior with an attitude. If he is not, the behavior is not likely to occur.

Now let us examine one of the objectives in detail, leaving the reader to conduct a similar exploration with the others at his convenience. The second item in the skill column reads "In Group Problem-Solving." This falls within the inner circle on our map (Figure 6) regarding interpersonal relationships. The full objective reads as follows:

> The learner will appraise the adequacy of his . . . group problem-solving skills and contrive a plan for establishing, and establish . . . such skills . . . which are culturally appropriate to his sex, appropriate to his developmental level, self-enhancing, and either neutral or beneficial to the larger society . . . Such skills should be adequate in dealing with . . . peers of own sex, peers of opposite sex, and adults.

The specific skills needed by the child have not been delineated. A teacher committed to these global objectives, however, would be pressured to define and nurture such skills as "defining the problem," "neutralizing threatening group behavior," and "building consensus."

This book stresses the development of behaviors in a life-like setting. The essential, isolated building-block objectives are determined by analyzing the pupil's performance in the more gross activities. Simulation is a key strategy in both instruction and evaluation. Traditional practices of drill and study are often called upon, but only in areas indicated from the child's inadequate

Figure 7

GLOBAL OBJECTIVES FOR A SOCIAL STUDIES CURRICULUM (K-9): BEHAVIORS WHICH ENABLE THE LEARNER TO LIVE WITH PEERS, TO LIVE IN HIS CULTURE'S INSTITUTIONS, AND TO NEGOTIATE EITHER AS AN INDIVIDUAL OR AN INSTITUTION MEMBER WITH OTHER MORE REMOTE INSTITUTIONS WHICH INFLUENCE HIS LIFE.

GLOBAL SOCIAL BEHAVIORS

INTERPERSONAL RELATIONSHIPS: THE LEARNER WILL: Appraise the adequacy of his interpersonal social relationships and contrive a plan for establishing and establish, adequate social relationships with associates in each of the following groups who are:

1. culturally appropriate to his sex,
2. appropriate to his development level,
3. self-enhancing, and
4. either neutral or beneficial to the larger society:

    PEERS OF OWN SEX
    PEERS OF OPPOSITE SEX
    ADULTS

    REPRESENTATIVES OF CULTURE'S INSTITUTIONS WHICH HE IS LIKELY TO CONTACT

INSTITUTIONAL RELATIONSHIPS: THE LEARNER WILL: Appraise the adequacy of his ability to deal successfully with cultural institutions with which he is affiliated and contrive a plan for establishing, and establish, functional relationships with each of the following institutions and/or components which are:

1. culturally appropriate to his sex,
2. appropriate to his developmental level
3. self-enhancing, and
4. either neutral or beneficial to the larger society:

SKILLS

THE LEARNER WILL: Exhibit skills in each of the following media with a competence appropriate to his sex and developmental level:

    IN GAMES
    IN GROUP PROBLEM-SOLVING
    IN DRESS AND GROOMING
    IN SOCIAL COMMUNICATION
    IN SOCIAL GRACES

    IN INSTITUTIONAL RITUALS AND ACTIVITIES
    IN GROUP PROBLEM-SOLVING
    IN DRESS AND GROOMING
    IN SOCIAL COMMUNICATION
    IN SOCIAL GRACES

THE LEARNER WILL: Exhibit skills in each of the following media with a competence appropriate to his sex and developmental level:

CONCEPTS

THE LEARNER WILL DESCRIBE:

The importance of social contacts in human living.

The importance of scientific advancement and education on ways of living.

ATTITUDES

THE LEARNER WILL: Inhibit responses in a group which will be either self-deflating, threatening to others, or prevent the group from reaching its goals.

THE LEARNER WILL: Maintain his integrity by dressing, speaking and behaving in a manner which is in harmony with his values and acceptable to the larger society.

FAMILY
SCHOOL
NEIGHBORHOOD

LAW AND MORES
FOLKWAYS

SPIRITUAL
INSTITUTIONS

DEMOCRATIC
GOVERNMENT

PUBLIC PROPERTY
PRIVATE PROPERTY
OTHER CULTURES
OTHER GOVERNMENTS
PRIVATE ENTERPRISE
PUBLIC ENTERPRISE

RELATIONSHIPS BETWEEN INSTITUTIONS: THE
LEARNER WILL: Appraise the adequacy of his ability
to affect the policy of the institutions to which he
belongs and contrive a plan for, and remedy, his
institutional behaviors so that the institutions will deal
more effectively with other institutions with overlapping and conflicting interests:

1. with a degree of proficiency appropriate to
    his developmental level;
2. in a manner which is self-enhancing;
3. the resultant of which is either neutral or
    beneficial to the larger society.

IN GAMES
IN GROUP PROBLEM-SOLVING
IN DRESS AND GROOMING
IN SOCIAL COMMUNICATION
IN SOCIAL GRACES
IN ECONOMIC TRANSACTIONS

IN DISCRIMINATING BE-
TWEEN ACCEPTABLE AND
UNACCEPTABLE BEHAVIOR

IN EMPATHIZING WITH
INSTITUTION'S WAYS

IN USING CHANNELS TO
INFLUENCE POLICY

IN USING INQUIRY SKILLS,
MASS MEDIA, MAPS,
CHARTS, GRAPHS, ETC.,
TO COLLECT INFORMA-
TION, ORGANIZE AND IN-
TERPRET ABSTRACT IDEAS

ALL ABOVE SKILLS ARE RE-
QUIRED.

The effect of moral
and spiritual values
upon human behav-
iors.

Ways of improving
family life, community
living, and national
and international wel-
fare.

The ways in which
communities, states
and nations are becom-
ing increasingly inter-
dependent.

THE LEARNER
WILL: Actively sup-
port the aspects of his
culture's institutions
which contribute to,
and move to modify
the aspects which inhi-
bit, the welfare of its
members as well as the
welfare of those indi-
viduals influenced by
the institution.

THE LEARNER
WILL: Identify with
and participate in insti-
tutions which support
his interests and val-
ues.

THE LEARNER
WILL: Inhibit behav-
iors which violate his
integrity and commit-
ments to the institu-
tions.

performances in the simulator.

A key emphasis is the nurturing of attitudes that will trigger the appropriate performances when they are needed in the real world. This is most likely to happen when the real world is simulated and the learner is rewarded for appropriate performances. With the group problem-solving objectives in question, the teacher should provide opportunities for the learner to meet in groups of his own sex, in groups made up predominantly of the opposite sex, and in groups with adults, if such instructional transfer is thought desirable.

Adapting the Objectives to a
Grade, Age, or Developmental Level

In any blueprint of objectives for life behaviors, we encounter the same difficult problem—that of defining the criteria for evaluation of a pupil's performance. The problem is somewhat obscured by our practice of wading through chronologies of America in the fifth, eighth, and eleventh grades, and of chronologies of the world in the fourth, sixth, and tenth grades. In such courses we avoid the problem of appraising the learner's ability to perform social behaviors by asking him instead to tell time by the chronologies we have presented. The student gets only one chance at this "concentration game." Since the test appears immediately after the game, his gaming skill can be readily judged.

However, if we wish instead to appraise the child's ability to establish healthy social relationships with his peers, we need other criteria. We must consider his developmental level and his available peers. The effective teacher must be alert to the varying social needs of each child and must modify instruction and evaluation procedures to meet these needs.

A checklist is one approach to identifying the needs and appraising the progress of a class. To use this technique, the teacher would have to be competent in appraising the adequacy of social behaviors of the age level with which she was working. (Such ability should be a requirement for entry into the teaching profession.) Here we might ask a teacher to check off from a series of adjectives those most descriptive of a Little Leaguer's baseball-catching ability or small-group "small-talking" ability.

The second method of evaluation of social behaviors is much more difficult and might require the services of a professional testmaker. This method calls for precise descriptions of expected behaviors along a developmental sequence. Timetables have been constructed for locomotor development, speech development, play development, physical development, and many others. These timetables have been based upon the occurrences of the behavior in large population samples.

Let us consider a seventh grade social studies teacher, blocking out a year's objectives for members of a class. Let us assume that the cumulative records of the class are truly records, and contain the answers the teacher needs about each child's progress. Perhaps the first question she will ask is, "Are his relationships with peers and adults mutually satisfying at a level commensurate with his ability?" If the answer is "yes," then the teacher can ignore development in this area for a time, because society will tend to reinforce these behaviors in the child's day-to-day living. If the answer is "no," the teacher must analyze the behavioral shortcomings of the child and provide experiences to remedy the situation. If the boy cannot play baseball, basketball, football, etc., well enough to participate with his friends, he must either learn these skills or learn a compensatory set of behaviors which can provide a medium for social satisfaction. It is the social studies teacher's responsibility to help the learner acquire the skills he needs for social development. The same applies to ability to perform graciously in a problem-solving group, in conversation, and in grooming himself for a social gathering.

Another student's problem might lie elsewhere than in the realm of inadequate skills. His attitudes or conceptualizations might not be sophisticated enough to enable him to adapt successfully. If this is the case, then the teacher must concentrate here.

Fortunately, there is much overlapping of problems, so many of them can be attacked with large-group instruction. When the problems are restricted to one or two persons in the class, programmed self-pacing materials are often available and effective. When these fail, individual programs must be tailor-made.

Education as a profession is coming of age. The time is ripe for the professionals within a school system to devise objectives, curricula, and evaluation procedures which really speak to the needs and achievements of the local community. A school district should know how its students compare in basic skills with others in the nation, but it should guard against using these data to fabricate a "mass man."

The "starter set" of behavioral objectives defined here can help in developing a vital social curriculum. Such a program aims at developing effective, contributing citizens whose social encounters are mutually self-enhancing to the participating individuals and institutions.

CHAPTER FIVE

BEHAVIORAL OBJECTIVES FOR THE DEVELOPMENT OF COMMUNICATIONS BEHAVIORS

Communications is one of the four basic problem-solving domains used in this book to delineate the behavioral needs of the growing child. While the child acquires a large portion of his communications skills through his interactions with others in out-of-school institutions, the school has the task of refining and polishing these performances. Communications refers to the meaningful messages one sends or receives. Such messages can be sent with careful deliberation or can be sent in spite of the sender's intent to hold them back—as in slips-of-the-tongue.

The most commonly used media for communications are the spoken and written word. The skills areas needed for transmitting these messages are speaking and writing, and those needed for receiving messages are listening and reading. This is not to say that there are no others. Facial expression, body movement, graphic and sculptural expressions, and musical expressions are but a few.

Apparently, the most popular containers for the school's communications curriculum are "language arts" and "English," with supplementary support coming from "speech" and "business." Elementary school teachers would have little difficulty shifting their allegiance from a language arts to a communications container but the secondary school teacher might find it quite difficult. There is a lack of agreement among English teachers as to the behaviors they are seeking. While some teachers are totally committed to teaching an "appreciation of literature," others are committed to "learning about the structure of the language" or "creative writing." Such diverse, narrow emphases permit learners to complete a high school course without guided learning experiences in listening, informative writing, recreational reading, conversational speaking, etc. A primary commitment of the school is clearly to nurture the learner's communications skills, and a major portion of this assignment should fall upon the language arts or English specialist.

A language arts teacher who is a literature specialist might very well be committed to some of the self-actualization objectives (see Chapter Six) as well as those in communications. This book is not advocating that a teacher or department in a school have sole rights to instruction in one of these problem-solving domains. Each school would have to appraise its instructional talents, and assign major responsibilities for particular objectives to those most capable.

With this general orientation, let us look to our map for identifying objectives for a communications curriculum. Figure 8 portrays the individual as a sender and receiver of oral and written messages. The speaking and listening media (centered) are by far the most used and their skills most needed. Our society, however, demands that all learners develop competencies in all four media. Unfortunately, in most schools the listening and speaking skill development is left to the home and neighborhood.

The learner portrayed moves about in five arenas. That is, he must deal with persuasive communications, informative communications, socially stimulating and gratifying communications, communications related to transacting business, and communications related to knowing and enhancing one's self.

Figure 8

The Learner's Communications World

The persuasive arena refers to convincing someone to take a questionable position or course of action. A learner should acquire skill in persuading others through writing and speaking that his needs and ideas merit consideration. The accompanying listening and reading skills might be called critical listening and critical reading. Here the individual learns to evaluate the arguments of another and respond appropriately.

Informative communications are concerned with the giving and receiving of information with a minimum of emotional accompaniment. This might include anything from asking or giving the time of day to doing library research or presenting an informative lecture.

The business and consumer arena deals with behaviors required of a citizen transacting business as either a buyer or seller in an efficient, congenial, and legitimate manner.

The social arena focuses on the effectiveness of the four communications media in building and maintaining satisfying social relationships. An interesting problem might arise here if a student who spoke "the King's English" moved into a new neighborhood where his peers frowned upon his speech patterns. A conscientious teacher might find it necessary to remove some of the polish. A skill useful to most individuals is the ability to modify speech patterns so as not to alienate an audience.

The self-actualizing arena (see Chapter Six) focuses on the learner's ability to communicate with himself and others in a manner that will enhance his self-confidence and self-picture. Included here might be creative writing, recreational reading, play-going, etc., where the focus is upon "knowing himself."

Many adults appear to graciously operate in these arenas with automated and unconscious behaviors. They write, speak, listen, and read with no apparent thought or concern. From where did this behavior come?

Operant conditioning research demonstrates that one can be taught to write, speak, listen, and read without concern for the formal teaching of concepts and generalizations about the skill.

First grade teachers will testify to the fact that many children suddenly "learn to read," and then many of the conceptual crutches atrophy.

This chapter is built around the position that the school's task is to develop problem-solvers—individuals who can communicate simple messages with a minimum of effort, and complex messages using all the problem-solving skills at their disposal. Certainly, reading and listening are automated skills for most educated adults when the message is simple. However, when the words get sophisticated and the author gets cunningly persuasive, the receiver needs as many cognitive handles as he can get on the medium to keep his bearings .

Hence Figure 8 pictures the communicator with a collection of automated or semi-automated skills, together with a collection of supportive cognitive maps and concepts to chart his course through rough waters. He needs techniques for identifying an adversary's motives, for reading between the lines, for accurately recalling what was sent, etc.

The rest of the communication world map is concerned with attitudes. This is probably the most difficult challenge for the teacher—transfer of training. We want the learner to *use* the behaviors we teach him, when he needs them in the real world. Probably the most effective way to teach these attitudes is to simulate the real world in the classroom and to monitor the performances. Our purpose in this chapter, however, is simply to identify an objective, not provide an instructional method.

Figure 9 (a, b, c, and d) presents an extensive list of language objectives, both terminal and transitional, which might be appropriate for a learner of average semantic ability—a chart which fleshes out the structure described in Figure 8. The row labeled APPLICATION describes the major arenas of Figure 8. The CONCEPTS, SKILLS, and ATTITUDES identify more specific responses likely to be essential in the performance of the application response at the appropriate time. A more extensive list of objectives would define the foci of a comprehensive

Figure 9a

ATTITUDES

Listening Attitudes:
The learner will:
Use the appropriate concepts and skills in his daily performance of developmental tasks.

SPECIFIC SKILLS

Skills Related to Informative Communications:
The learner will:
Identify main ideas, sequences of ideas, and details, and make two-point outlines when appropriate.
Systematically identify and use appropriate references in pursuit of information.

Skills Related to Persuasive and Editorially Biased Communications:
The learner will:
Identify the speaker's intent and mood, and attitude toward the subject.
Discriminate between relevant and irrelevant ideas.
Discriminate between fact and fiction.
Draw inferences using cause-effect relationships.
Compare two or more speeches for relative reliability on facts, bias, and currency.

Recreational and Aesthetic Skills:
The learner will:
Identify a variety of listening areas which interest him.
Specify procedures he can take to find interesting listening in each area (above).
Identify times in his schedule when he can get recreational materials and use them.

GENERAL SKILLS

The learner will:
Produce the 40 basic English sounds when presented with the spoken letter or digraph.
Recall and interpret sentences immediately after he has heard them.
Identify relationships between ideas he has heard.
Discriminate facts from fiction and from opinion in his listening.
Summarize what he has heard.

CONCEPTS

Concepts:
The learner will describe:
the importance of communications to the self.
the importance of communications to society.
the importance of communications to society's institutions.
the impact of scientific advancement on the media we use to communicate.
the ways in which the motives of men affect the communications they send and receive.
the techniques of deception in communications.
the difference between the free and controlled association of ideas and how a good communication requires both.

APPLICATIONS

LISTENING: The learner will translate, interpret, and extrapolate from formal and informal oral statements in the form of:
Informative Communications: with a degree of proficiency appropriate to his developmental level, and he will seek out such communications when life-problems require it.
Persuasive Communications: with a degree of proficiency appropriate to his developmental level.
Editorially Biased Communications: with a degree of proficiency appropriate to his developmental level.
Recreational and Aesthetic Communications: with a degree of proficiency appropriate to his developmental level, and he will seek out such communications when life-problems require it (self-actualization concerns).

Figure 9b

ATTITUDES

Reading Attitudes:
The learner will:
Use the appropriate concepts and skills in his daily performance of developmental tasks.

SPECIFIC SKILLS

Skills Related to Informative Communications:
The learner will:
Identify main ideas, sequences of ideas, and details, and make two-point outlines when appropriate.
Systematically identify and use appropriate references in pursuit of information.

Skills Related to Persuasive and Editorially Biased Communications:
The learner will:
Identify the author's intent and mood, and attitude toward the subject.
Discriminate between relevant and irrelevant ideas.
Discriminate between fact and fiction.
Draw inferences, using cause-effect relationships.
Compare two or more sources of information for relative reliability on facts, bias, and currency.

Recreational and Aesthetic Skills:
The learner will:
Identify a variety of reading areas which interest him.
Specify procedures he can take to find interesting books in each area (above).
Identify times in his schedule when he can get recreational materials and use them.

GENERAL SKILLS

The learner will:
Produce the 40 basic English sounds when presented with the printed letter or digraph.
Read words using phonics, context clues, and recalled sight words.
Recall and interpret sentences immediately after he has read them.
Discriminate facts from fiction and from opinion in his reading.
Summarize what he has read.

CONCEPTS

Concepts:
The learner will describe:
the importance of communications to the self.
the importance of communications to society.
the importance of communications to society's institutions.
the impact of scientific advancement on the media we use to communicate.
the ways in which the motives of men affect the communications they send and receive.
the techniques of deception in communications.
the difference between the free and controlled association of ideas and how a good communication requires both.

APPLICATION

READING: The learner will translate, interpret, and extrapolate from formal and informal written statements in the form of:
Informative Communications: with a degree of proficiency appropriate to his developmental level, and he will seek out such communications when life-problems require it.
Persuasive Communications: with a degree of proficiency appropriate to his developmental level.
Editorially Biased Communications: with a degree of proficiency appropriate to his developmental level.
Recreational and Aesthetic Communications: with a degree of proficiency appropriate to his developmental level, and he will seek out such communications when life-problems require it (self-actualization concerns).

Figure 9c

ATTITUDES

Speaking Attitudes:
The learner will:
Use the appropriate skills and concepts in his daily speaking encounters.

SPECIFIC
SKILLS

Skills Related to Informative Communications:
The learner will:
Communicate his desires in a socially acceptable manner to appropriate persons when in need of assistance or information.
Communicate appropriate responses to requests from others for information.

Skills Related to Persuasive Communications:
The learner will:
(Within a moral or ethical framework) convince others to modify their behaviors to incorporate his needs or the needs of the larger society.

Skills Related to Social Communications:
The learner will:
When the occasion arises, engage in social conversation with both peers and adults in a manner which is mutually satisfying to the participants.

GENERAL
SKILLS

The learner will perform the following skills in a manner appropriate to his developmental level. Skills in:
accurately producing language sounds
pronouncing and using words
effectively phrasing ideas
organizing communications
producing effective voice quality
effective delivery

CONCEPTS

Concepts:
The learner will describe:
the importance of communications to the self.
the importance of communications to society.
the importance of communications to society's institutions.
the impact of scientific advancement on the media we use to communicate.
the ways in which the motives of men affect the communications they send and receive.
the techniques of deception in communications.
the difference between the free and controlled association of ideas and how a good communication requires both.

APPLICATION

SPEAKING: The learner will translate, interpret, and extrapolate his own experiences and observations in:
Information Spoken Communications: which communicate with a degree of proficiency appropriate to his developmental level.
in a culturally appropriate manner commensurate with his developmental level.
Persuasive Spoken Communications: which persuade with a degree of proficiency appropriate to his developmental level.
in a culturally appropriate manner commensurate with his developmental level.
Social Spoken Communications: which communicate with a degree of proficiency appropriate to his developmental level.
in a manner which is self-enhancing.
in a manner which enhances the speaker's social stimulus value in the eyes of the recipients.

Figure 9d

ATTITUDES   *Writing Attitudes:*
The learner will:
Use the appropriate skills and concepts in his daily writing encounters.

SPECIFIC   *Skills Related to Informative Communications:*
SKILLS   The learner will:
Communicate his desires in a socially acceptable manner to appropriate persons when
     in need of assistance or information.
Communicate appropriate responses to requests from others for information.

Skills Related to Persuasive Communications:
The learner will:
(Within the moral or ethical framework) convince others to modify their behavior to
     incorporate his needs or the needs of the larger society.

Skills Related to Social Communications:
The learner will:
When the occasion arises, correspond with friends in a manner which is mutually
     satisfying to the participants.

Recreational and Aesthetic Skills:
The learner will:
Use all of the above writing media in a manner which is self-enhancing.
Identify and use for creative purposes writing media which are suitable to his abilities
     and provide for creative expression.

GENERAL   The learner will perform the following skills in a manner appropriate to his
SKILLS   developmental level. Skills in:
     producing legible letters and words rapidly
     producing appropriate words
     phrasing communications
     organizing communications
     editing products for public consumption which are free from errors in:

spelling	format
redundancies	punctuation
irrelevancies	facts
grammar	

CONCEPTS   *Concepts:*
The learner will describe:
     the importance of communications to the self.
     the importance of communications to society.
     the importance of communications to society's institutions.
     the impact of scientific advancement on the media we use to communicate.
     the ways in which the motives of men affect the communications they send and
       receive.
     the techniques of deception in communications.
     the difference between the free and controlled association of ideas and how a
       good communication requires both.

APPLICATION   *WRITING:* The learner will translate, interpret, and extrapolate his own experiences
     and observations in writing through:
     Informative Communications: which communicate with a degree of proficiency
       appropriate to his developmental level.
       in a culturally appropriate manner commensurate with his developmental
       level.
     Persuasive Communications: which persuade with a degree of proficiency
       appropriate to his developmental level.
       in a culturally appropriate manner commensurate with his developmental
       level.
     Social Communications: which communicate with a degree of proficiency
       appropriate to his developmental level.
       in a manner which is self-enhancing.
       in a manner which enhances the writer's social stimulus value in the eyes
       of the recipients.
     Creative Expressions: in a manner which is self-enhancing and possibly in a
       manner which is educational.

collection of daily lesson materials for a school's language-arts program. Most of these objectives would fall under one of those on the chart.

This four-page figure should be useful as a guide in selecting experiences and materials for a communications program to insure its comprehensiveness. A modification might have to be developed for low-verbal learners, but this chart should suggest its content.

The advantages of such a definitive structure are many:

1. Both the forest and the trees can be seen in a single glance.
2. A finite, comprehensive list of objectives can be delineated.
3. A program based upon such a format can be systematically evaluated.
4. A common core of terms and organizers can be used in developing writing, speaking, listening, and reading concepts and skills.

Other communications media could be incorporated, but these four are most basic. Recent concerns over non-verbal communications raise interesting questions, but these can probably be best considered as auxiliary media. Non-verbal communications are most significant when their messages are in conflict with the meanings conveyed verbally. One might have to attend to non-verbal cues in critically evaluating a communication or in sending an involved communication. The medium, however, could seldom be called primary.

Many teachers will view the format suggested here as a Utopian pipedream, while for others it will be a viable option. To some it would be sacrilegious to demean the study of literature by relegating it to "an aesthetic communication to be received" status. Others would view it as a meaningful, integrating transition. Perhaps the model simply takes a little "getting used to."

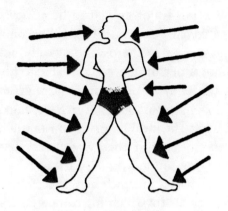

CHAPTER SIX

BEHAVIORAL OBJECTIVES FOR THE NURTURING OF A SELF-ACTUALIZING INDIVIDUAL

The term "self-actualization" was coined by Kurt Goldstein (1939). He noticed as he worked with brain-damaged soldiers that they tended to reorganize their psycho-physical capacities to make the result both more functional and more satisfying. Since World War II many phenomenologists—Abraham Maslow and Carl Rogers among them—have used the concept of self-actualization as a foundation stone to their therapies and to their proposed solutions to many of the world's social and educational problems. Self-actualization occurs *within* the individual himself. He experiences self-actualization as he participates in creative, problem-solving activities which demand and get his wholehearted participation and yield adequate, self-satisfying solutions. The individual experiences a feeling of self-assurance and an increased confidence in his ability to master future, related problems; an observer views the individual as increasing in poise, grace, confidence, and efficiency. If the behaviorist needs an external measure for the evaluation of his successes, he will have to derive it from inferences based upon these observations.

Self-actualization is not an end to be achieved, but a process to be participated in. Combs' (1962) "becoming" process is related to an awareness in the psychologically healthy child that he is evolving into a person more acceptable to himself than what he was. In this awareness of becoming, one experiences self-actualization. The Shangri-la is never reached, but is successively approximated, while the ideal model is constantly being revised.

In this sense, then, in theory, self-actualization can be a continuous state for an individual participating in challenging, problem-solving activities in which he is successful and in which he is aware of the degree to which his competencies are increasing. Every individual has some problem-solving media within which he can be especially creative, and others where creativity is unlikely. It is with the discovery, and nurturing, of these self-actualizing media that a well-defined portion of the school curriculum should be concerned. Let us seek a perspective for building a curriculum which will nurture attitudes and skills and educate self-assured problem-solving people. The global objectives of this curriculum are capsuled below.

Self-Actualization Objectives

As a result of the school's self-actualization curriculum, the learner will:

1. Identify several specific media in each of four media clusters—social, communications, environmental, and aesthetic—which have the potential for him as media for self-actualization.

2. Demonstrate his competence in manipulating the elements of each selected medium so that while the medium continues to challenge him he is also able to have sufficient success to bolster his self-confidence and self-esteem.

3. Periodically schedule involvements with these media in his daily living so that he reacts to challenge with self-confidence and self-assurance.

4. Describe and defend his short- and long-term program for using the media to maintain his self-confidence and self-esteem.

We are assuming that the school should help every child to develop competencies in self-actualization media which he can call upon to recover from defeats, to order his world, and to give him the confidence to take on leadership roles.

Robert Havighurst's (1953) concept of the developmental task suggests many activities which can be self-actualization media for at least some learners. (See Chapter One.) Developmental tasks, such as learning to walk and talk, learning to read and write in middle childhood, learning to converse with individuals of the opposite sex in adolescence and adulthood, are supportive to many learners but might be useful for self-actualization only during the rudimentary learning stages. For instance, the first grader typically rejoices in every reading victory. However, as he comes to realize his limitations, the medium loses its potential for self-actualization. Later, however, he might pick up a facet of a former childhood medium (e.g., reading) and develop it into a supportive medium (e.g., reading historical fiction about early America). The little child who bangs on a pan as he parades may later find satisfaction in developing skill on a musical instrument. A teacher aware of the potential of classroom activities and skills for self-actualization, and the inclinations of certain individuals for certain kinds of activities, can do much to vitalize learning in the classroom and nurture self-confident, self-assured, gracious citizens. The media which are supportive throughout the life span probably deserve considerably more attention than the school typically gives. Examples of such media are story telling, volunteering, gift giving, etc.

The adequacy of such a school program could be appraised by the activities the child engages in during his free time both as a child and as an adult, the vocation he elects, and the degree to which he is able to maintain a confident, self-assured demeanor throughout daily frustrations.

Figures 10 and 11 picture the citizen as living in four problem-solving domains—social, communications, environmental, and aesthetic. These have been selected both because they roughly

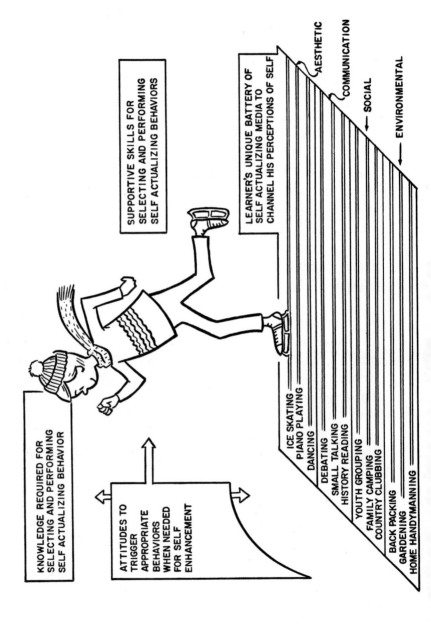

Figure 10

The Self-Actualizing World
of the Learner

Figure 11

Focusing on Media
for Self-Actualization Emphasis

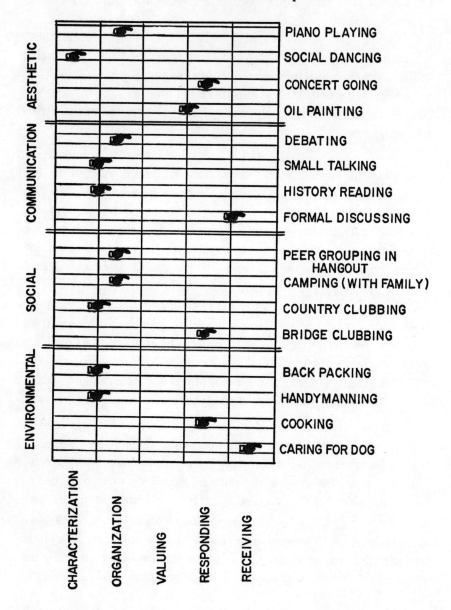

follow the basic subject matter divisions of the public school and because they cover quite comprehensively the problem-solving concerns of man.

Figure 10 portrays these areas with a few potentially self-actualizing media. The channels identify media to which the individual can frequently go to restore his sense of well-being (for instance, the good skater can take to the ice to restore his confidence in his physical prowess). Let us examine each of the problem-solving areas.

1. *Social.* Civilized man is a social creature. Everyone must encounter his social world and solve problems related to his interactions with it. Each successful encounter will increase his confidence in the success of the next encounter. Social contacts can have self-negating or self-actualizing consequences. A learner should be helped to identify the social patterns in his environment which provide for his own self-actualization so that he can increase their frequency and perform effectively when involved. The adolescent portrayed in Figure 10 puts in five or six hours a week with a group of peers in a neighborhood hamburger hangout. In addition, he enjoys outings with his family and activities with his peers at the country club. These are social self-actualizing media for him. There are countless possibilities for other social media, but most of them would not be appropriate for him.

2. *Communications.* Man, with his ability to use language, is unique among the animals, and many people feel that someone who cannot communicate is only part human. Writing, speaking, listening, and reading are the core media clusters of communication, but the individual media under each are extensive. The adolescent portrayed here belongs to the school debate team, is an entertaining small-talker, and reads widely in history. These provide him with a supportive communication field to nurture his confidence and self-esteem in his daily communications problem-solving.

3. *Environmental.* Anthropologists frequently list as man's

greatest gift, next to language, his thumb-finger opposition—a characteristic which enables him to manipulate the physical world to serve him. Man spends a great deal of time in such pursuits. The confidence and self-esteem of many are enhanced by their successes, but the confidence and self-esteem of others are depressed by their inadequacies. We cannot expect to make manipulative geniuses out of learners who are "all thumbs" by increasing their confidence. However, it is possible to help them discover their strengths and nurture them in appropriate activities. The young man portrayed gets his environmental problem-solving self-assurance from his backpacking, gardening, and handymanning pursuits.

4. *Aesthetic.* The aesthetic category is removed from man's practical world and consists of media which can provide effective and extended sources of "soul food." Media are available for people of all ages, from mudpie making and finger painting to crocheting and story telling, and for all levels of sophistication, from painting by the numbers to sculpturing stone. All require a degree of skill which makes the performance challenging but allows for success after a struggle. A distinction must be made here between the aesthetic act of the self-realizing child and the aesthetic act of the recognized artist. John Dewey (1916) defined education as "that reconstruction and reorganization of experience that adds to the meaning of experience and directs the course of subsequent experiences." This definition also defines the aesthetic act within the self-actualization framework. The individual reorganizes his past experiences in the act and emerges with a new, functional perspective. If this emerging perspective is new to a child, he has perpetrated an aesthetic, self-actualizing act—but probably not one worthy of display in a museum. Only if the work organizes the world artistically for a segment of the art-loving public is it worthy of a place in the museum. It is certainly possible for an individual to invent his own private and unique aesthetic medium which works for him, but it is also certain that the vast majority will use media developed and

transmitted by the culture. Learners should be helped to find a few aesthetic media which they can tap for self-actualization. Figure 10 shows the youth supported by his skating, piano-playing, and social-dancing pursuits.

The reader should not assume that all traditional rudimentary skills and knowledge are to be eliminated from the curriculum in favor of self-actualization concerns. Havighurst's developmental task orients us to all the basic skills the child needs to live in a complex society. The citizen certainly needs to talk, read, write, calculate, use geographic, political, and economic concepts, manipulate his physical environment, etc. At certain stages in the child's development he becomes aware of these needs and can be self-actualized as he increases his competencies. This will occur, however, only if the learning is attempted after the need is felt and before an alternate behavior has been learned to reduce the tension caused by the need. Thus the task of mastering functional, traditional skills is not incompatible with the self-actualization focus but is actually vitalized and enhanced by it.

However, when the individual reaches a level of competency in a medium commensurate with the demands placed upon him by the society, the medium loses its potential for self-actualization. At this point he may either specialize in the medium, developing it into one which can continue to harness his energies and continue to provide support, or he may move to another medium that can provide these advantages.

Actually, the school has been responsible for only a few of the media used by the adolescent in Figure 10. Ideally, the school should have helped him more. The learner probably simply stumbled upon most of these media. Certainly, some traditional school subjects, such as creative writing, chemistry, and wood-shop, can serve to orient the child to self-actualizing media. The boy on the map (Figure 10), as he encounters daily frustrations, has supportive channels available to him where he can be "recreated" in a 30-minute skate or a two-week backpacking trip.

A Model for Viewing an
Individual's Self-Actualization Milieu

Four media clusters for self-actualization have been examined—social, communications, environmental, and aesthetic. We must help the individual understand the self-actualization value of a medium to encourage him to nurture his own unique collection of competencies. A five-part taxonomy is used here as an intensity hierarchy scale. Figure 11 adds to the information in Figure 10 an intensity dimension. After the intensity scale has been described, a third hierarchy—Maslow's (1954, 1968) hierarchy of human needs and motives—will be added to form the cubical model found in Figure 12.

The Intensity of Affective Involvement. Teachers are seldom aware of the degree of commitment they are seeking when they teach attitudes. They nurture attitudes of thrift, but they don't want misers. They nurture attitudes of cleanliness, but they don't want compulsive bathers. They pressure all eighth graders to paint, but they don't expect them all to become Rembrandts.

David Krathwohl, in the *Taxonomy of Educational Objectives: Affective Domain* (1964), describes a five-step hierarchy of involvement. The taxonomy focuses on a learner's attitude toward a person, place, thing, idea, or behavior. Typically, as he becomes familiar with it, he will develop a patterned way of responding to it. The first phase is distinguished by his noticing the referent when it enters his environment—*receiving*. The second phase is distinguished by his *responding* or reacting to the referent. For instance, a boy might notice a bird building its nest in the back yard (receiving). He may or may not interrupt his activity to watch it more closely. The third phase, *valuing*, implies that the learner considers the object of more than momentary value or as something worth preserving or *valuing*. For instance, the child might buy a book on the nesting habits of birds. The fourth phase, *organization*, implies that the learner builds the interest into his routines to insure its repetition. Our bird-watcher might join a

Figure 12

A Model for Viewing
an Individual's Self-Actualization Milieu

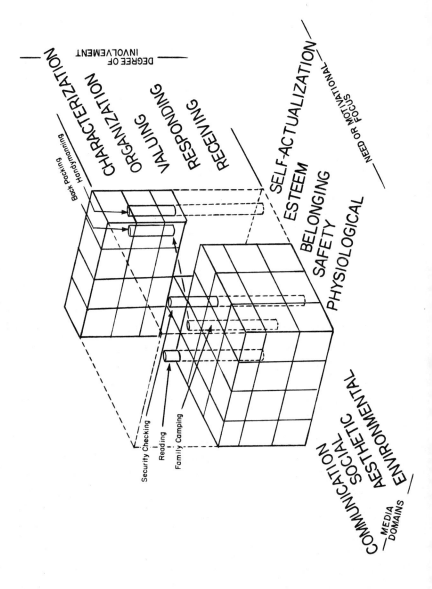

bird-watching club which meets every Saturday afternoon. The fifth phase, *characterization*, is distinguished by the dominant role the relationship plays in the life of the learner. Here our bird-watcher might commit himself to make ornithology his life's work.

The vertical dimension (receiving, responding . . .) in Figure 11 uses this hierarchy. The boy portrayed has built into his life at the organizational level, or above, two aesthetic media—piano playing and social dancing; three communications media—debate, reading, and small-talking; three social media—peer grouping in hangout, family camping, and country clubbing; and two environmental media—backpacking and handymanning.

A school interested in nurturing self-actualizing youth would do well to work with them in developing uniquely appropriate profiles and helping them to acquire the skills, attitudes, and knowledge needed to call upon the media for recreation.

Let us now move on to Figure 12, *A Model for Viewing an Individual's Self-Actualization Milieu.* Two of the three categories defined by the axes have already been explained in detail. The third follows.

The Individual's Motivational Concerns. Maslow says that motives change in a patterned manner as man matures as an individual and as a society organizes itself to provide for the needs of its members. The individual tends to be consumed by a particular cluster of needs until he is satisfied they will be met. He then moves on to focus firmly on the next cluster of needs. The following ladder sketch portrays Maslow's hierarchy of needs:

Certainly a young, isolated, hungry, cold, or pained child (physiological needs) is not likely to be captivated by social small-talk (belonging need) or water-color painting (self-actualization). A child who had been in such a state for a prolonged period would probably first want assurance that it wouldn't happen again (a safety concern) before becoming socially involved. Hence the Maslow argument that the steps must be taken one at a time—that the need structure is hierarchical. Let's look at the separate categories.

Physiological concerns are the primary concerns of the infant, the extremely poor, the combat infantryman, the Arctic explorer, etc. When individuals do not have adequate resources to maintain their physiological needs of body temperature control, body chemistry, and freedom from pain, these concerns become dominant. Research in human needs indicates other "musts" which we often fail to note. One needs sensory stimulation (possibly a rudimentary aesthetic need), fondling (possibly a rudimentary communications need), and a chance to manipulate things once he is physiologically able (possibly an environmental need).

Safety concerns become an individual's focus when, though his physiological needs are met, he fears the satisfactions will be short-lived. One must develop a "basic trust" (Stone and Church, 1957) that his world is supportive. The stutterer and the "miser" are often manifestations of safety concerns in communications and environmental spheres.

Belonging could be called "feeling comfortable and effective in the medium." One can feel comfortable with paint, letter writing, a tea party, driving a car, or driving a nail.

Esteem is a social term. Americans belong to an extremely socially oriented culture, and their concern for social recognition often motivates them to acquire the additional competencies needed to make a medium a suitable channel for self-actualization. For instance, the individual seeking esteem might put forth the added effort required to play an instrument in an orchestra, pitch on a baseball team, or get a bid to a fraternity.

An individual's *self-actualization* channels are diverse, not because the self is divided, but because self-confidence, self-esteem, and a feeling of self-realization are reached through diverse media. It is likely, too, that self-confidence is confined to particular fields of action for most individuals and is not generalized. The generalization process, in any event, will be left for the therapist. The school can only lead the learner to particular media, nurture his participation in them, and encourage him to extend his use of them beyond the school wall and years. Jung (De Quenetain, 1961) argued that his "individualized" man emerges only through extended psychoanalytic confrontation. His ideal does not appear appreciably different from Maslow's self-actualized man. The reader will note that the rear right-hand face of the cube (Figure 12) is identical to Figure 11.

Voids in the Cube: Approximately half the cells in the cube have relevance to the self-actualization process. The avowed objectives of most schools can be corralled into the large low-involvement mass that consumes two-thirds of the total occupied volume of the cube. Here are the knowledge, skill, and attitudinal elements required for minimal "good citizen" behaviors. A graduate with such a background could take care of his own communications, social, aesthetic, physical, and environmental needs below the self-actualization level and would also be concerned with keeping up with the Joneses. However, such an individual's attitude toward himself would be governed by the chance happenings in his environment and his successes or failures in coping with these confrontations.

The self-actualization media identified in the back face of the cube are those which the individual can call upon for supportive, confidence-building experiences, placing his attitudes toward himself at least partially under his own cognitive control. In some cases the foundation skills and attitudes essential for satisfying experiences in these media are established as the individual tries to master simple behaviors concerned with lower-level needs. In other cases, either where the lower-level learning activities are fragmented or where attitudes toward them are negative, a new foundation has to be built to support the activities.

A concern for an activity at an organizational or characterizational level, when the activity provides little psychological support, is ridiculous. In fact, this might prove to be another approach to a definition of neurosis. Consider, for example, the person who overuses such defense mechanisms as overcompensation, scapegoating, rationalization, etc. The model identifies an individual who spends forty minutes every evening checking the screens, doors, windows, and burglar alarms in his home for fear that the safety of his worldly goods is in jeopardy.

The tubes in the model identify prototypic patterns of media which people attempt to use for self-actualization. We have already mentioned the security-conscious individual who is overly concerned that he will lose his personal environment. The medium might have been supportive, and even self-actualizing, to the individual as he learned to respond to, value, and provide for his personal possessions. He has now, however, become overly consumed with an activity which has lost its supportive capabilities.

The reading commitment at the organizational level occurs when the learner recognizes his reading shortcomings and plans a remedial program to correct them. This temporary involvement might be a more gruelling than self-actualizing experience. There might be a momentary reward at the end if all goes well.

A portion of the knowledge, skills, and attitude roots for the home handymanning medium were cultivated as our subject tried to satisfy his need to keep his room and toys in reasonable order. His father abdicated the handyman role when he had a heart attack during the child's adolescence. As the boy improvised solutions while waiting for the service man to appear, he discovered he liked the role and assumed it. His father's psychological support and occasional advice enabled him to shore up his position in the medium until he acquired the necessary skills. If the family can supply this support, the medium can have self-actualization potential. If it cannot, the activities are likely to be perceived as burdensome chores.

The backpacking medium has at its foundations the family camping experiences of childhood, and is finally sparked by a family overnight hike up Bald Mountain. Here he recognizes that backpacking gives him the feeling that he "has the world by the tail."

Therefore, although most of the cube might at some time be frequented by an individual, less than half of it (the two large blocks) has potential for self-actualization.

The following six generalizations can guide the classroom teacher in helping the individual to identify, nurture, and use effective self-actualization media.

1. Every individual has a unique profile of media with potential for self-actualization.

2. As an individual matures in a school setting attuned to his needs, he should acquire the behaviors he needs with few discipline commitments above the responding and valuing levels.

3. If the individual has difficulty with certain behavior mastery, he might need to make a temporary commitment at the organizational level which he would abandon when the objective is reached.

4. The only motivational level with lasting potential for self-actualization is the self-actualization slice of the cube.

5. Individuals who become overly engrossed in physiological, safety, belonging, and esteem concerns—engrossed beyond the responding and valuing level—are likely to be frustrated in their self-actualizing pursuits.

6. Every individual should be helped to acquire a proficiency in, and an attitude toward, several media in each media cluster which have the potential for nurturing his self-actualization and which he will call upon to serve this end.

Figure 13 identifies global objectives in each of the four media clusters which can serve as the focus for a self-actualizing curriculum. In each cluster the learner is expected to:

1. Identify several media in which his participation enhances his perceptions of himself and his functional efficiency.

2. Recall the knowledge essentials for a creative performance in each of the media.

3. Master the skills of each medium to the extent that he can

Figure 13

Guide for Identifying Specific Objectives for a General Education Curriculum Nurturing Self-Directed, Self-Actualizing Individuals

Domains to be Mastered	Aesthetic	Communications	Social	Environmental
Knowledge expected of individual in each domain.	*The learner will:* 1. identify several aesthetic media where his participation enhances his perceptions of himself and his functional efficiency. 2. recall the knowledge essentials for a creative performance in each of the aesthetic media.	*The learner will:* 1. identify several communications media where his participation enhances his perceptions of himself and his functional efficiency. 2. recall the knowledge essentials for a creative performance in each of the communications media.	*The learner will:* 1. identify several social media where his participation enhances his perceptions of himself and his functional efficiency. 2. recall the knowledge essentials for a creative performance in each of the social media.	*The learner will:* 1. identify several environmental media where his participation enhances his perception of himself and his functional efficiency. 2. recall the knowledge essentials for a creative performance in each of the environmental media.
Skills expected of individual in each domain.	*The learner will:* Master the skills of each of the above media to the extent that he can use them creatively to formulate new perceptions.	*The learner will:* Master the skills of each of the above media to the extent that he can use them creatively to formulate new perceptions.	*The learner will:* Master the skills of each of the above media to the extent that he can use them creatively to formulate new perceptions.	*The learner will:* Master the skills of each of the above media to the extent that he can use them creatively to formulate new perceptions.
Attitudes expected of individual in the monitoring and modifying of his self-perceptions.	*The learner will:* Recall and use appropriate aesthetic media to enhance his self-confidence and esteem when his lowered efficiency requires it.	*The learner will:* Recall and use appropriate communications media to enhance his self-confidence and esteem when his lowered efficiency requires it.	*The learner will:* Recall and use appropriate social media to enhance his self-confidence and esteem when his lowered efficiency requires it.	*The learner will:* Recall and use appropriate environmental media to enhance his self-confidence and esteem when his lowered efficiency requires it.

use it creatively to formulate new perceptions.

4. Recall and use appropriate media to enhance his self-confidence and esteem when his lowered efficiency requires it.

The model is simple and descriptive of the process by which man has acquired recreation skills throughout the ages. The question is, can a school curriculum provide the learner with a functionally comprehensive battery of skills and attitudes strong enough to elicit self-actualizing behaviors when they are needed? Every generation nurtures the behaviors in some individuals; can a curriculum be devised to provide them for *everyone?*

CHAPTER SEVEN

BEHAVIORAL OBJECTIVES FOR
"HARNESSING ONE'S PHYSICAL ENVIRONMENT"

Science educators typically assume that the way to teach children to make their environment work for them is to teach them the mysteries, the attitudes, and a capsuled version of the bodies of knowledge of the sciences. It is taken for granted that if one "studies biology" he can raise healthy plants and animals, and if he "studies about laws of mechanics" he can do mechanical things. One might quite legitimately ask the question, "Might it not be better to groom a child's plant- or animal-raising ability, or groom his mechanical facility, interjecting concepts only when they apply to the ongoing process?"

As we have said, general education refers to the educational objectives needed by the learner for fulfillment as a person and as a member of society. It does *not* refer to those objectives which are vocationally oriented or are prerequisites to vocational training. The academic subjects pursued in the elementary and early secondary school—science, mathematics, grammar, and social studies—are neither purely general education nor purely vocational education. Some learners find history and mechanics "soul food," qualifying them as general education. Others who are not excited by them see them as tools for their future vocational life. Most students, however, are "turned off" by them and will ultimately declare that they belong in neither category.

This chapter is an attempt to map the functions of an adequate general education program in environmental problem-solving and to identify sample instructional objectives in the functional area depicted.

Perhaps one of the most comprehensive and empirical attempts to define man's relationship to his environment is J.P. Guilford's research (1967) on the structure of the intellect. This structure portrays a plausible framework showing how man's knowledge is related to what he can do and what he can produce. He identifies three major dimensions of human abilities:

1. The ability to store information about one's environment (content).
2. The ability to make specific elements in one's environment work for him in specific ways (products).
3. The ability to perform certain operations using stored content in the process of contriving products (operations).

The following diagram oversimplifies Guilford, but might make his three dimensions more vivid.

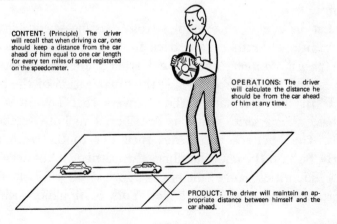

CONTENT: (Principle) The driver will recall that when driving a car, one should keep a distance from the car ahead of him equal to one car length for every ten miles of speed registered on the speedometer.

OPERATIONS: The driver will calculate the distance he should be from the car ahead of him at any time.

PRODUCT: The driver will maintain an appropriate distance between himself and the car ahead.

Here we have a man standing in his demanding world where he must *produce.* He has a lifetime of stored *content* knowledge which he may, or may not, be able to recall when demands are made upon him, and he has a battery of *operational* skills at his disposal. Living requires that he cope with his world. His natural abilities in combination with his past experiences, however, might not have equipped him to handle the multitude of diverse tasks life demands of him.

Three rather obvious foci for an environment-based curriculum are evident for the student portrayed. The teacher can:

1. Try to fill him with understandings (tell him how to drive).
2. Try to develop process skills (teach him component processes like division and judging distances).
3. Try to teach him to produce the specific products (actually an infinite number) which the world will demand of him (put him in a variety of cars and let him perform on a variety of roads under many conditions).

There are blends of these; but typically teachers, syllabi, curriculum packages, and schools have biases—where one of these foci defines the curriculum structure, while the daily ingenuity of the teacher is relied upon to provide appropriate amounts of the other two.

Let us cite some examples from existing science materials. The traditional textbook approach found in most schools focuses upon *verbal content*—upon the learner's ability to recall and comprehend principles governing the organization of the physical world. In this orientation the "powers that be" in a school purchase a text series which is distributed to both teachers and pupils. The "better" text series spell out to the teacher in an orderly fashion the understandings the learner will master. The list below identifies some major categories of content deemed important by the makers of a New York State junior high school science syllabus (New York State Education Department, 1956):

> Kinds of Living Things
> Keeping Healthy
> Using Electricity
> Lifting and Moving Things
> Common Chemical Changes
> Energy from the Sun
> The Atmosphere
> The Earth and Sky
> Rocks and Soil
> Survival of Living Things

The understandings which provide the backbone of the curriculum are in the form of verbal principles. For instance, the first five of the eighteen understandings specified under the Rocks and Soil category (listed below) are typical:

1. Rocks are continually being worn away by weathering, steam action, abrasion, and other agents.
2. Rocks are formed and reformed by weathering, erosion, and transportation of sediments.
3. The past history of a rock can often be learned by examining it carefully.
4. Artificial rocks are made from materials obtained from natural rocks.
5. Remains and imprints of plants and animals that lived long ago are often found in sedimentary rocks.

If the teacher is to make these concepts clear, she must introduce facts, processes, and products.

The *operations* or *process* approach is epitomized in the American Association for the Advancement of Science's *Science: A Process Approach* (1968). In these materials the following process behaviors are nurtured:

General Processes	Science-Based Processes
Observing	Experimenting
Using Space/	
Time Relationships	Interpreting
Using Numbers	Formulating Hypotheses
Measuring	Controlling Variables
Classifying	Defining Operationally
Communicating	
Predicting	
Inferring	

These focus on the orderly behaviors exhibited by the individual as he systematically attacks and solves his environmental problems within a scientific perspective. This approach is clearly process oriented.

The experimental approach epitomized by the Elementary Science Study (1966) "Behavior of Mealworms" package stresses the value of spontaneous, unprogrammed inquiry. The pupil begins his study of mealworms with undirected observations. He may place the worms in a box near a light, in a maze, or in a group. As his interest is stimulated, he will begin to experiment, generalize, and predict. The inquiring student appropriately stimulated will pursue only relevant (to him) questions and fundamental concepts and behaviors based upon his own understandings. Hopefully, then, a cross-sectional sampling of packaged life-experiences will produce a learner with the problem-solving experience needed to cope with his world at his stage of development. If these experiences were simulated life-experiences (which they are not), numerous, and random, the *product* concerns would probably be adequate.

These three perspectives are quite diverse and yet identify characteristics which should be incorporated into any instructional program. One cannot learn to predict, measure, or even observe as the process approach seeks to teach, without concepts and comprehensions. One cannot learn to predict the weather without knowledge of how atmospheric pressure, temperature, cloud cover, topographical features, etc., affect weather. Neither can an instructional program without captivating experiences which stimulate inquiry be very effective. *All* the emphases must be included.

Figure 14 pictures the learner living in eight environmental complexes with which he must come to terms. There is nothing sacred about either the number or nature of the complexes. In most large secondary schools you could find one or more courses in each area, attesting to the reasonableness of the foci. Let us briefly define and examine each, recognizing that other adequate though quite different batteries could be devised.

1. *Physically Maintaining a Home*: Everyone, at times, is responsible for the maintaining of a shelter or a home. Whether it be a tent or an estate, it requires a systematic approach to cleaning, preserving, lighting, heating, replacing, storing, etc. Whether the occupant performs the work required or hires someone to do it, he should have a rudimentary knowledge of the problems likely to be encountered and the solutions likely to be effective. One could predict from the cultural and socio-economic background of the learner whether it would be more feasible to nurture functional physical skills in the home-maintaining operations or to nurture efficiency in sub-contracting for the services.

2. *Managing of Personal Transportation System*: Home garages in all socio-economic classes often contain large assortments of vehicular, aquatic, and airborne modes of transportation—mini-bikes, motorcycles, snowmobiles, automobiles, trucks, boats, helicopters, etc. In addition we rent cars, ride in taxis, busses, trains, and planes. The maintenance, management, and financing of a personal transportation system is often the major frustration of a family.

3. *Preparing and Storing of Food*: There might never have been a time when the average citizen knew less about the preparation and storage of food than he does now. Packaged, preserved, ready-to-serve foods of questionable nutritional and

Figure 14

*Objectives Concerned with
Harnessing One's Physical Environment*

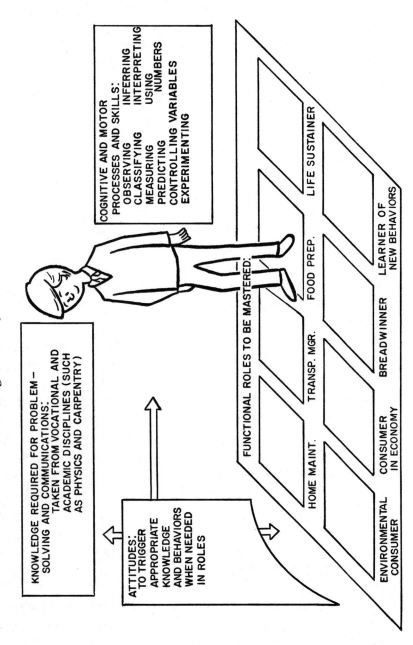

aesthetic value are the staples of the home. A family spends 5 to 10 percent of its waking hours at the table and a homemaker spends an additional 10 to 15 percent of her time in the preparation, storing, and disposing of foodstuffs. From both a nutritional and self-actualization vantage point, skilled performances in this area can change the tenor of a sizable portion of the family's day. (This complex could be combined with "Physically Maintaining a Home," No. 1 above.)

4. *Sustaining Plant, Animal, and Human Life*: Everyone, at times, is responsible for the physical care of a garden, a lawn, a house plant, a pet, a family, or at least himself. The concern, as with the other complexes listed here, is not viewed in terms of principles known, or separate process-related skills perfected, but in terms of the state of the product being cared for.

5. *Consuming and Preserving the Environment*: The ecology movement of the late 1960s brought to light the impending danger to the environment from an overabundant, careless populace. Forests, soil, and mineral resources are being depleted, air and water are being polluted, and refuse is everywhere. An educated citizenry is lauded as the cure-all. The writer argues, however, that the danger will not be averted by the dissemination of platitudes and understanding. Overt behaviors and even life styles must be changed.

6. *Efficient Buying of Consumer Goods*: As the advertiser is getting more proficient in his business, so must the consumer if he is to meet his needs and balance his budget. He must learn both to identify quality products and to detect deceptive packaging. Probably our two greatest uses for mathematics are in measurement and monetary concerns. Experiences in consumer buying would greatly strengthen these skills. In addition, the learner should develop the ability to appraise the quality of goods and services.

7. *Earning a Living*: Every youth should enter the economic world with a collection of behavior competencies which are in perennial demand and which capitalize on the learner's potential.

This means that a student recruited to play professional football should also have the behaviors required for employment when injuries or aging make it necessary to leave football.

8. *Learning Functional Behaviors*: No school program can, or should, try to teach a learner all he will need to know for a lifetime of problem-solving. Rather, the learner needs enough basic skills in a variety of areas so that he is confident in his problem-solving abilities. In addition he must have the confidence and skills necessary to supplement his knowledge as he attacks new problem situations. There is some question as to whether this should be an eighth territory on our map or a subdivision under each of the other seven.

These eight life-centered complexes are offered as a conceptual base upon which to build an environmental problem-solving curriculum. They are practical because we already think this way, and related simulated learning activities are easy to contrive.

The first row of Figure 15 restates the roles to be mastered in the eight environmental complexes we have suggested.

The second row of the figure focuses on the knowledge expected of the role players. Perhaps auto mechanics, homemaking, and consumer economics are the only existing curricula that remotely define a preparation for these roles, and these are typically designed for only the non-academic students. Traditionally the school has taken the easy route and boiled down the academic disciplines into units of instruction. Fifty years of such teaching, however, testifies to the fact that such knowledge does not automatically become functional when one assumes one of these eight roles. A Boy Scout handbook listing merit badge requirements for plumbing, carpentry, cooking, pioneering, etc., might provide us with a better base than existing curricula. (Incidentally, these requirements have been stated *in behavioral terms* for over fifty years.)

The third row is concerned with the skills required of the role players. Only one or two skills have been spelled out for each role, where in reality there would be many. The skills would vary from

Figure 15

Guide for Identifying Behavioral Objectives for a General Education Curriculum Focusing on Environmental Problem-Solving

ROLE TO BE MASTERED ↑	HOME MAINTENANCE MANAGER	HOME TRANSPORTATION MANAGER	PREPARER AND STORER OF FOOD	GUARDIAN OF PLANT, ANIMAL, HUMAN LIFE	CAREFUL ENVIRONMENT CONSUMER	CONSUMER GOODS PURCHASER	FAMILY BREAD-WINNER	LEARNER OF FUNCTIONAL BEHAVIORS
KNOWLEDGE EXPECTED OF ROLE PLAYER	*THE LEARNER WILL:* Explain the dangers involved in using volatile, flammable cleaning agents in the home. Explain how a home's wiring dictates the appliances which can be used in a given location. Etc.	*THE LEARNER WILL:* Devise an appropriate annual maintenance schedule for a year-old car. Describe in detail the steps to be taken to store a motor vehicle or boat for the winter. Etc.	*THE LEARNER WILL:* Given the contents of a home freezer and the knowledge that the current has been off for a five-day period, describe and justify a salvage procedure. Explain the common causes of milk spoilage and suggest controls. Etc.	*THE LEARNER WILL:* Identify the life-sustaining needs of an infant human, a dog, and a geranium. Etc.	*THE LEARNER WILL:* Explain, with examples, why government regulations are often necessary in conserving an life-supporting environment. Etc.	*THE LEARNER WILL:* Describe the distinguishing characteristics of new durable fabrics and how they can be distinguished from the less durable. Etc.	*THE LEARNER WILL:* At any time in his school career, identify several occupations for which he has potential with respect to interest and ability and appropriately defend his selections. Etc.	*THE LEARNER WILL:* Given an environment problem he has the need and the potential for solving, acquire the knowledge necessary for adequately performing the task. Etc.
SPECIFIC SKILLS EXPECTED OF ROLE PLAYER	*THE LEARNER WILL:* Light and adjust pilot on gas furnace. Replace worn cord on table lamp. Replace two foot section of broken, concrete sidewalk. Replace broken window. Replace washer in leaky faucet. Etc.	*THE LEARNER WILL:* Maintain air pressure in tires of family car. Change tire on family car. Start car with rundown battery using booster battery. Replace worn windshield wiper blade. Etc.	*THE LEARNER WILL:* Store foods in appropriate locations in family refrigerator, capitalizing on accessibility, temperature, etc. Given the meat dish for a family meal, plan and prepare a nutritional, appetizing meal. Etc.	*THE LEARNER WILL:* Plant and cultivate several tomato plants producing an average yield of ten edible tomatoes. Etc.	*THE LEARNER WILL:* Devise a detailed implementable plan for reclaiming a section of land in the community. Etc.	*THE LEARNER WILL:* Given comparable products in different sized containers in a supermarket, select (or purchase) the "best buy." Etc.	*THE LEARNER WILL:* Appear punctually for commitments and special appointments. Regularly identify and master skills requisite to vocational goals he has tentatively selected. Etc.	*THE LEARNER WILL:* Given an environment problem he has the need and the potential for solving, acquire rudimentary skills necessary for adequately performing the task. Etc.

GENERAL PROCESS SKILLS EXPECTED OF ROLE PLAYER

The Learner Will in His Problem Solving Efforts in Each of the Above Roles Use the Following Processes Effectively:

GENERALIZED PROCESSES		SCIENCE BASED PROCESSES
Classifying	Observing	Experimenting
Predicting	Using Numbers	Interpreting
Inferring	Measuring	Controlling Variables
Using Space/Time Relationships		Defining Operationally

ATTITUDES EXPECTED OF ROLE PLAYER

The Learner Will Recall and Use Appropriate Knowledge, Skills, and Behaviors (Listed Above) When Needed in His Environmental Problem Solving community to community as climates, foods, vocations, etc., differed.

The fourth row focuses on the generalized skills which cross role lines. Only those developed in *Science: A Process Approach* have been cited, but this list could be extended. One must be cautious in assuming that these processes generalize automatically. For instance, an adolescent pitcher skilled at predicting the base-running inclinations of his opposition need not be skilled in predicting his behavior under the influence of drugs.

The fifth row centers on the attitudes required to elicit the appropriate role behaviors. Every behavioral component requires an affective component if it is to be retrieved when it is needed. Throughout the learning sequence, therefore, considerable attention must be given to broadening the stimuli that will elicit the behaviors taught.

To develop a functional curriculum out of these schemata would require facilities not found in the typical school, but yet not so foreign that they are unknown in a nearby metropolis. For instance, a school could have one or more run-down houses, a run-down farm, and a few near-junk automobiles which it is refurbishing and which it will later sell to redeem its investment. These three kinds of facilities would cost the community little or nothing and would provide the base for the major portion of the program.

Curriculum materials would have to be designed which zeroed in on the typical storage, ecology, maintenance, etc., problems one is likely to encounter and which would provide for the nurturing of the content and process base required to produce the needed repairs or modifications. As individuals or small groups would be effecting these changes, most of the instructional materials would have to be self-pacing and individualized.

The task of designing such a curriculum and developing the curriculum materials is a big one and one that only a sizable school district could manage without outside help. Education is at a crossroads, however. The family, church, and neighborhood are not nurturing the functional skills the way they once did, while at the same time the mass media are doing a pretty good job of disseminating discipline-based knowledge—once the primary role of the school. The schools must redefine "general education" and tool themselves for the task of developing confident, competent individuals who can make their environment serve them, yet preserve the environment so it can serve others.

The first draft of such a curriculum will not be Utopian. Only through continued refinements will the materials, teachers, and learners be able to maintain the cutting edge needed for orienting the learner to his role as an environmental consumer.

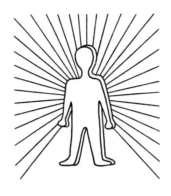

PART III

BRINGING ABOUT THE CHANGE

CHAPTER EIGHT

The foregoing chapters have focused upon four maps—social, communications, self-actualization, and environmental—which can help educators chart a contemporary curriculum in general education to serve both learner and society. We have witnessed in the twentieth century a change in the general education role of the school. Formerly the school was guardian of the "3 R's" competencies of the citizenry. Now it must complement the family, neighborhood, and other public educational agencies in developing the functional behaviors of the child. The school has shown its acceptance of this challenge by including new offerings such as sex education, driver education, and vocational homemaking, and in the platitude-like objectives stated in elementary school teachers' manuals and syllabi. Nevertheless, a traditional curriculum format borrowed from the college and academy still dominates public education. The slack left by the deteriorating traditional educational institutions of the family, neighborhood, and church is not being taken up by the school, and we are all feeling the tremors caused by the resulting chaos.

The academic disciplines, focusing upon the culture's store-houses of knowledge and inquiry skills, provided acceptable school subject foci in a stable culture, but are quite unsatisfactory in a chaotic field.

The program offered here is based upon the points explored in preceding chapters. The task of this chapter is to bring together the keystones in the program, to isolate some of the barriers to their implementation, and to suggest some approaches to the overcoming of the barriers.

1. General education curricula should focus upon behavior clusters needed by a learner to gain the support of his social and physical environment and to provide similar support to others.

2. Comprehensive maps of the learner's environmental, problem-solving world should be charted by teachers as vital guides to make their educational world dynamic and meaningful to both themselves and their pupils.

3. The profession's conception of an ideal learning environment must be changed from a quiet, authoritarian classroom to a laboratory where the learner spends most of his time in either a real-life or simulated environment, *solving problems.*

4. The techniques of the behavioral technologist must be ordered and taught to the profession, so teachers will be able to nurture the development of problem-solving skills in the life-centered school laboratory.

5. Extensive curricular materials must be developed, catalogued, and made accessible to the teacher to nurture core behaviors in the classroom so that the teacher can have models for developing other units and time for working with individuals.

6. The knowledge, skills, and teaching style competencies of existing faculties must be identified and exploited when designing an educational system. To use a teacher as a pawn in a system is to capitalize on only a small fraction of his potential. A relatively stable transactional curriculum is needed which will allow time for curricular materials to be developed and teachers to graciously

change.

7. While the teacher must feel he is free to use his talents creatively in the structuring of learning experiences for his pupils, he must work as a member of one or more educational teams to cooperatively nurture learner growth in an efficient manner and to convey needed educational innovations from their introduction to their institutionalization.

8. The community and the educational hierarchy must be educated along with the classroom teachers, and their energies and resources enlisted, if such programs are to become operational.

The Clusters and the Maps

The old scope and sequence chart of the traditional curriculum structure served a purpose. It identified for the teacher and the administrator a content presentation schedule which insured that every child in the system was exposed to a comprehensive collection of content in an order which appeared logical—at least to an adult. While the scope and sequence chart is not a viable model for a functional behavior-based instructional system, such a system does require organizational charts. The educator and the learner need a map by which they can identify their strengths and weaknesses, and *developmental scales* with which they can measure progress. This book has presented four such charts, and the scaling concern was discussed.

One should not consider these to be the ultimate in curricular maps. They are simply first steps which have been smiled upon in the early 70s. Better maps will and must emerge.

The Learning Environment

Most educational theorists and researchers since E.L. Thorndike and Charles Judd (1908) have agreed that functional problem-solving behaviors are developed by using a mix of realistic practice and intermittent periods of conceptualization. While some learners require more practice than others, all need it in large doses.

The recent simulation explosion has capitalized on the transfer of training research. A wide variety of games, mock-ups, dramatic structures, laboratory packages, etc., has been marketed to provide captivating media to hold the learner through sequences of practice and conceptualization.

Public education has been slow to utilize these materials and insights, probably because most schools are still focusing upon the acquisition of knowledge and paper-and-pencil skills rather than real-life skills, and so simulation of life situations appears irrelevant.

If general-education-focused institutions could shift their allegiances to the functional objectives described in the text of this book, simulation would become the backbone and the glue in the new instructional system.

Behavior Modification

Seventy years of behavior modification theory and research have made little impression on the structure of public education. E.L. Thorndike, J.B. Watson, and B.F. Skinner, to name a few, endorsed the notion that one's present behaviors have been derived through an interlocking sequence of reinforcements stemming from the reflex behaviors emitted at birth. The infant simply responded to his environmental stimuli with crude, reflexive behaviors. These behaviors were, in turn, either reinforced, ignored, or punished—either by people or by their perceived effectiveness in helping the individual to adjust to environmental pressure. The reinforcement pattern programmed into his environment molded his sophisticated adult behaviors. Most of the new behaviors were shaped without the learner's awareness, while others were at least partially under cognitive control.

This learning process, now called operant conditioning, accounts quite adequately for most of the functional learning required of an effective problem-solver.

An educational system focusing upon functional global

behaviors and operating within a largely simulated setting is ideally suited to a "behavior modification" reinforcement system. Reinforcements such as teacher and peer approval, gratifications resulting directly from problem solutions, and material rewards could be quite effective. Most of these would be automatically dispensed in the game or simulated social structure and would not require elaborate bookkeeping systems.

A Materials-Based Program

The nurturing of functional behaviors requires materials considerably more elaborate than the traditional textbook. The learner must play the role of a problem-solver in life-like situations and be appropriately reinforced for his responses. This implies the need for nearly self-contained learner packages capable of sustaining learner interest and insuring the vigilant maintenance of reinforcers.

The teacher needs to match materials to learners and to supplement the materials where they prove inadequate. If good materials are not available, the system cannot work. One cannot deviate far from a lock-step system without good supporting, involving, sustaining, and reinforcing materials.

Faculty Competencies Shape the System

The nature of the viable model and the timetable for realizing such a model-based system depend upon the perspectives, the skills, and the teaching styles of the institution's instructional staff.

While the possession of adequate instructional material is a necessary condition for an effective general education program, it is not a sufficient condition. Teachers must be sold on the system and be "ready, willing, and able" to support the student operating within it. A "taught-to-the-tune-of-a-hickory-stick" teacher, a "rally 'round the flag" teacher, or a "good time Charlie" teacher will require a blend of job tailoring and retraining to make the transition. As we are currently slightly overstocked with teachers, a few can be replaced. However, the requirements of the transitional system must be such that our present instructional staffs with a moderate amount of retraining can operate well in the new system.

The "subject-matter authority" role held sacred in our traditional education becomes subservient to the "materials specialist" role, and the "educational guidance" role in functional behavior-based education.

A school interested in making such an educational transition must carefully appraise the teacher competencies it will ultimately need, the teacher competencies it has, and the teacher competencies it will need for the transition period where there will exist only mediocre materials and partially trained teachers. It must then chart a 5- to 10-year program defining intermediate instructional models, a material development plan, and a plan to maximize the use of faculty talents throughout the period.

The Team as the Change Agent

Educational change can only be brought about through an extensive team effort. Because of the widespread resistance to change from both within and without the educational establishment, a team effort is required to maintain the morale and fervor of the team members and to assure them they are not working alone. A new applied behavioral science of "organizational development" has recently emerged with some tools for building and maintaining team organizations. If schools could use these tools, the movement to make public education functional would be greatly enhanced.

Enlisting the Support of the Establishment

When asked by a teacher how to change curricula with a traditional administration balking at every request, the writer often responds with, "Close your door and let your imagination and conscience be your guide." While this advice might be useful in germinating and incubating innovations, it contributes little to the nurturing of an educational structure. For the latter task, research and developmental efforts in a community can combine contemporary refinements in the art and science of teaching with the personnel and material resources needed to improve the educational establishment. The leap from the innovative teacher behind a closed door to the effective and efficient system is a monumental one.

The key to a dynamic, functional educational system is a battery of effective teaching materials adapted to the behavior needs of the learner, the learning styles of the learner, and the teaching styles of the faculty, and also a system for adapting the materials to changing conditions. For centuries we have relied upon a few textbooks and a free-enterprise publishing structure to provide such materials which have, for the most part, been quite inadequate.

Let us detour for a moment to examine the power structure of the educational establishment (Figure 16) to identify some vulnerable points on which an attack could be focused.

In the educational structure of these United States there are many points at which curricular change can be initiated and from which it can be directed. These points include the individual classroom, the separate school building, the school system, the state education department, the U.S. Office of Education, the professional education association, the large publishing house, etc. Figure 16 may serve to order the educational structure of a typical state, pointing out both the legitimate and extra-legal avenues through which pressures to change or preserve curricula are applied. The federal Constitution clearly places the power to establish and regulate educational institutions in the hands of the separate states. Individual states might differ slightly from the pattern in the chart, but not appreciably.

The state board of public instruction, whose members usually have lengthy and staggered terms, and its chief administrator—the superintendent of public instruction or the commissioner—are the educational policy-makers for the state. They are sometimes

Figure 16

Pressures Influencing the Nature
of the Learning Experiences in the School

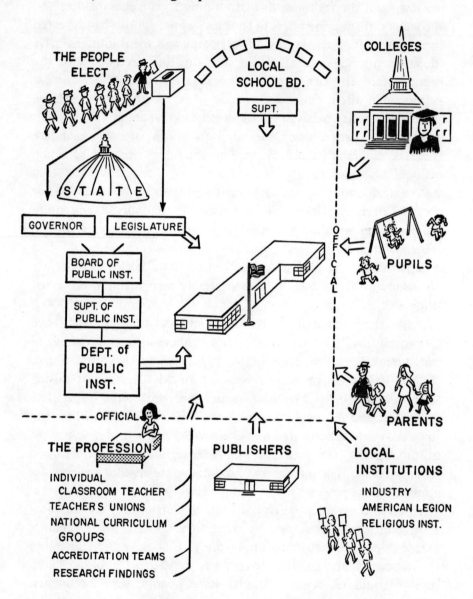

powerful, as in New York and California, and sometimes weak, as in Iowa and the Dakotas, due often only to the personalities and behaviors of their members in the past, whose actions have created precedents. In many states, these boards and their administrative departments mandate curricular patterns and textbooks for the entire state. In other states the separate schools are almost unaware of their existence outside of a record-keeping sphere. State legislatures occasionally drag educational policy-making into the political arena, using their appropriation powers to mandate courses and policies and to serve as watchdogs over the spending of public tax monies.

Local school boards vary greatly in their power to influence policy. In large cities they are often both political and quite autonomous, wielding power which influences the learning climate in individual classrooms. State courts, however, have not looked kindly on school boards which "buck" state policies, and their decisions in these areas almost invariably recognize the power of the state.

As the credentials of teachers and local administrators have improved over the last 100 years, policy-making decisions in instructional matters have gradually shifted to the professional. This shift leaves the non-professional boards the task of raising monies through taxation and keeping the profession frugal. The economic and political climate of the times determines where the monetary decisions are made. However, when decisions are disputed, the state courts and the legislative appropriations committees spring into action, and the state usually reclaims its constitutional powers.

Publishers are powerful shapers of curricula. Their publication policies are governed by what they consider to be salable. Their sales approach is to apply pressure at the most vulnerable points to sell the products they have decided to publish. These points could be school boards, state boards, superintendents, principals, or even classroom teachers. Often the act of purchasing a text is *in effect* the act of curriculum making.

Parents, industries, churches, unions, and other pressure groups can also apply pressures at the same decision-making points as the book salesman, although the points of vulnerability vary considerably from school system to school system.

Two remaining pressures not as yet mentioned are the learners in the classroom and the professional organizations of teachers. From these groups come the most profound guidelines. Curriculum groups from organizations such as the National Council for the Social Studies or the National Council of Teachers of English periodically publish well-thought-out curriculum specifications which are often adopted and disseminated by state and city departments of education and converted into texts by publishers. These pronouncements, though often unheralded, have widespread effects.

The child in the classroom plays an interesting role in curriculum development. This role can be considered either minor or major, depending upon one's definition of curriculum. If one considers the curriculum as the official study guide, or syllabus on the teacher's desk, the child's influence in its structure has been small. However, if one considers the scheduled learning experiences available to the child while he is under the jurisdiction of the school as the curriculum, then the child is a major determiner.

Consider the primary school child in his daily hour ride on the school bus being teased incessantly until he has learned to fear the school day and distrust society. Or consider the floating dice game occurring at noon every day where a school Mafia is systematically milking a few affluent but gullible peers. Or consider a few girls who, bored with study hall, organize a book club where each buys and reads a book and then negotiates exchanges with others until the good books have been read by all. These are all learning experiences, regularly scheduled along with those guided by the teacher. They are an operational part of the curriculum and might do more to shape the child's behavior than all the experiences specified in the syllabus. When the child joins an activity to fill a void in the "official" course of study, he has elected an option in the "real curriculum"—the "operational curriculum"—of the school. In this sense, then, the child influences curriculum. In fact, when a teacher builds on the child's natural bents in the classroom, she is working with the child in shaping curriculum.

From the above discussion we can identify five fortresses where systematic curricular change can be effectively carried on:

1. The state department of public instruction, where the legitimate powers rest, but which is often far from the classroom where the implementation must take place.

2. The professional teacher organizations, whose current thrusts, unfortunately, are usually in the form of salary demands.

3. The local school district, with its professional resources, its laboratory, its limited funds, and its hourly need for programs.

4. The U.S. Office of Education, with its financial resources and resource people, but no grass roots and no legitimate power.

5. The publisher, with a pay-as-you-go financial structure and no direct contact with the school and the child.

They all have the following: personnel committed to the development of effective educational programs; a continuing existence, making them amenable to working toward long-range goals; professional perspectives which can identify and enlist additional personnel capable of engineering such developments; and a stability which could assure those with financial resources that they can handle the job.

Two ingredients, however, seem to be missing—blueprints describing the greener pastures and the working relationships which must exist between the classroom teachers and the developmental agencies in the designing and building of the curricular materials. This book has described the greener pastures; let us now look at the classroom teachers.

The Classroom Teacher's Role in
Curriculum Design and Development

The traditional role of the teacher in the public school has been to establish and maintain a learning climate which will wed the curriculum materials of the classroom to the learners, maximizing the need fulfillment of the learner. The good teacher was, and is, essentially a well-informed classroom manager. It is true that some teachers made their own curricular materials, some used the community as a laboratory, and others used no curricular materials at all, but the classic pattern—followed in the vast majority of the nation's classrooms—has been dominated by prescribed textbooks or learning packages which provide the continuity and content for instruction. The teacher's task was to make the content interesting, to involve the student, and—if possible—to make the learning functional.

The focus throughout this book implies an instructional system which allows for large-group, small-group, and individualized learning geared to the developmental needs of the learners. It implies the existence of instructional materials that are far more sophisticated than traditional materials, because the teacher must manage several packages at one time, while formerly she had only to manage one.

The task of producing such materials is two-faceted. First, there must be a logistical concern for systematically developing a comprehensive collection of materials to meet the learning needs likely to be encountered in the typical classroom. Second, there must be a concern for the developing of sophisticated materials which are almost self-supporting. While the specialist is needed as the mainstay in the design operation, the resourceful, inventive teacher with a flair for writing is the keystone of the material-developing operation. The reality-based teacher, faced with the need for functional materials for tomorrow morning, is best equipped for the writing operation. A half-time teacher writing two or three instructional packages might be assigned to a group for a two-month period, writing, revising, and field-testing with each group, emerging with a finished product at the end of the year. (The author has developed a system for differentiating between the designer's and writer's roles and delineating a process by which they can work together [1971b].) Countless variations of this pattern could be devised to increase the productivity of the writer-teacher and to improve the quality of the product. Remember, the teacher being sought after as a materials developer is not typical. He is a good classroom manager, as are many of his colleagues, but he is more. He has conceptualized relationships which his colleagues react to automatically; he is analytical rather than spontaneous in his approaches to instructional problem-solving; he is well above average in his ability and willingness to write; and he has the drive to follow a writing task to completion.

The Transition

An optimistic estimate of the time required to make a need-based individualized instructional system operational would be ten years under ideal conditions. Most of the educational innovations of the past two decades were conceptualized, implemented, and died a natural death in less than half this time. These innovations tended to involve only a small segment of a faculty and only a minor portion of their time. Out of this major overhaul would emerge a new breed of teacher, a new curriculum with new objectives, learners with a new "modus operandi," and a new kind of curriculum materials.

Many of the characteristics of the new system are already determined. Individualized and small-group instructional materials will be available in quantity and quality beyond the fondest dreams of today's teacher. Bookkeeping systems for storing information about the learner and his progress and the curriculum materials will become sophisticated enough for the teacher to manage an individualized instructional program with no more effort than required in his present program. The teacher will play a role more like a good guidance counselor than a traditional teacher. Most of his time will be spent with individuals and small groups, tending to the process of learning and introducing learners to appropriate materials, rather than disseminating information.

Clearly we cannot set up such a school next fall and make it operational. We do not have the materials, the systems, or the trained teachers. Neither can we wait ten years for such elements to develop—because they will not. Materials and systems will be developed and published only if the profession is ready to assist in the development and then to try the product. Teachers will make the transition only gradually as they are weaned from their expository patterns and learn to see the worth of alternate approaches. The task of engineering the role transition from authoritarian to a more non-directive one is formidable.

Following are some guidelines which innovators might find useful in planning for educational change. They will provide the reader with a much-needed long-range perspective regarding a route to developing functional programs for tomorrow's schools.

Guideline 1. Transitional curriculum formats should be negotiated for as large a school district as possible to serve as the mainstream structure for from five to ten years. Such formats would of necessity have to allow the lecture-text teacher and the behavior-focused teacher to live under the same roof. The agreement would imply that:

a. Because our faculty members take a variety of philosophical and methodological positions on educational issues and because the arguing of the issues has precipitated irrational and erratic curriculum changes generating more heat than light, let us resolve to build a curricular format compatible with all our positions.

b. Such a format would have to have textbook or packaged materials which traditional teachers would feel comfortable with, would have to be concerned with content roughly compatible with the content specialties of the existing faculties, yet would have to survey the behaviors which the behaviorists are concerned with developing.

c. Auxiliary behavior-based packages of instructional materials would be developed which are compatible with the traditional materials and made available for all teachers. Teachers would be encouraged but not compelled to use them.

Man: A Course of Study or *Science: A Process Approach* might serve as examples of courses which teachers might live with for the ten-year transitional period. Both programs are discipline-oriented and acceptable to the traditionalist, yet they totally involve students, frequently putting them in positions which the behaviorist can capitalize upon.

Guideline 2. Hard-line, way-out philosophical and psychological positions should be avoided in pronouncements from the power structure—they tend to frighten and entrench teachers in extreme positions. Terms like behavioral objectives, operant conditioning, individualized instruction, programmed instruction, etc., have a messianic flavor for disciples but often a demonic flavor for others. The meaning of the terms in an elementary school setting is often quite different from that used in the laboratory of a behavioral psychologist. Terms like this are often used by administrators and teachers for their shock value or to impress. If we are to build on a consensus, we probably need to look for equivalent terms with more neutral connotations.

Guideline 3. The U.S. Office of Education, state departments of public instruction, local school districts, professional teacher organizations, and educational publishers must work individually and together to design, develop, test, and implement comprehensive curriculum packages. The task is staggering and commitment must be total. These agencies have not, as yet, recognized the problem. (See Drumheller, 1971b.)

Guideline 4. The profession should concentrate its efforts to get government and private funding agencies to give top priority to the development of supplementary, behavior-based instructional packages. The society and the individual have pressing needs for functional behaviors in youth that might determine the individual's chances of surviving. While not all teachers are either willing or able to work to such ends, the ranks of the capable are growing rapidly.

Guideline 5. School systems must work out systems for reinforcing teacher behavior that facilitates pupil learning. There might be some question as to which behavioral objectives should be given priority, but there is no debate regarding the teacher's assignment as a learning facilitator—the student must learn. The writer is convinced that if a teacher can concentrate on teaching students so that it makes a difference, he will be ready for a behavioral objective orientation.

Guideline 6. The public must be kept informed and included in the consensus of educational policies and practices. This does not mean that they have the power to make policy, but that schools must operate with the consent of the governed. Schools should never be surprised by public reaction. They should have their hands on the public pulse and should be constantly dialoguing with, listening to, and selling the public. The public is not the enemy of education but must be kept informed and enlisted or its wrath will be felt.

Conclusion

A public school curriculum built around the limited dreams of today's educational technologist would probably look ridiculous in 1980. A dream school with a completion date ten or fifteen years hence must be built in stages, with periodic opportunities for review and revision. The initial plan must be relatively loose and must be palatable to both the dreamers and the rank-and-file educators. As the rank and file hone their competencies and focus their dreams, a new revision of the possible will emerge which could not have been predicted a few years earlier. Adapting to classroom realities will require plan revisions, new alliances, new rallying cries, and some shifts in leadership. However, unless the movement is able to sustain its thrust, periodically correct its course, and avoid the schism of revolution, it cannot take root and grow.

Educational technology is young and its Utopian dreams, though exciting, are premature. Many of its rallying "principles" will not weather the next decade. A transitional school is a must and this book is offered as a guide for framing its objectives.

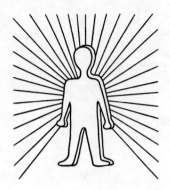

REFERENCES

American Association for the Advancement of Science. *Science: A Process Approach.* New York: Xerox Corporation, 1968.

Association of Teachers of Social Studies of the City of New York. *Handbook for Social Studies Teaching.* Third Edition. New York: Holt, Rinehart, and Winston, 1967.

Cole, Henry P. *Process Education.* Englewood Cliffs, New Jersey: Educational Technology Publications, 1972.

Combs, Arthur W. (Ed.) *Perceiving, Behaving, Becoming: A New Focus for Education.* Washington, D.C.: Association for Supervision and Curriculum Development, 1962.

Committee of the National Council for the Social Studies. The Role of the Social Studies. *Social Education,* October, 1962, *26,* p. 315.

De Quenetain, Tanneguy. What Has Carl Jung Left Us? *Realites,* April, 1961, pp. 42-49.

Dewey, John. *Democracy and Education.* New York: The Macmillan Company, 1916.

Drumheller, Sidney J. Behavioral Objectives for the Social Studies in General Education. *Educational Technology,* September, 1971, *11,* p. 31. (a)

Drumheller, Sidney J. *Handbook of Curriculum Design for Individualized Instruction: A Systems Approach.* Englewood Cliffs, New Jersey: Educational Technology Publications,

1971. (b)

Drumheller, Sidney J. Objectives for Language Arts in Nongraded Schools. *Elementary English,* February, 1969, *46,* p. 119.

Drumheller, Sidney J. The School's Responsibility to Society and to the Individual. *Educational Horizons,* December, 1967, p. 65.

Dyer, Henry S. Toward Objective Criteria of Professional Accountability in the Schools of New York City. *Phi Delta Kappan,* December, 1970, *52,* p. 206.

Elementary Science Study. St. Louis, Missouri: Webster Division, McGraw-Hill, 1966.

Goldstein, Kurt. *The Organism.* New York: American Book Company, 1939.

Guilford, J.P. *The Nature of Human Intelligence.* New York: McGraw-Hill, 1967.

Havighurst, Robert. *Human Development and Education.* New York: Longmans, Green, 1953.

High School Geography Project. *Geography in an Urban Age.* New York: The Macmillan Company, 1969.

Judd, C.H. The Relation of Special Training to General Intelligence. *Educational Review,* 1908, *36,* p. 28.

Krathwohl, David, Benjamin Bloom & Bertram Masia. *Taxonomy of Educational Objectives, Handbook II: Affective Domain.* New York: David McKay, 1964.

Maslow, Abraham. *Motivation and Personality.* New York: Harper & Row, 1954.

Maslow, Abraham. *Toward a Psychology of Being.* Second Edition. Princeton, New Jersey: Van Nostrand, 1968.

New York State Education Department. *Science 7-8-9.* Albany, New York, 1956.

Roselle, Daniel. Citizenship Goals for a New Age. *Social Education,* October, 1966, *30,* p. 415.

Sanders, Norris M. & Marlin L. Tanck. A Critical Appraisal of Twenty-Six National Social Studies Projects. *Social Education,* April, 1970, pp. 383-449.

Social Studies Curriculum Program of Education Development Center, Inc. *Man· A Course of Study.* Cambridge, Massachusetts, 1970.

Stone, L. Joseph & Joseph Church. *Childhood and Adolescence.* New York: Random House, 1957.

Taba Curriculum Development Project in Social Studies. Palo Alto, California: Addison-Wesley, 1965.

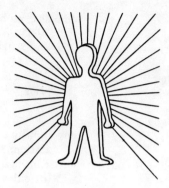

INDEX

DATE DUE